How to Start a
KETO DIET

**YOUR 21-DAY MEAL PLAN TO WEIGHT LOSS
WITH BASIC SIMPLE KETO RECIPES
PLUS SHOPPING LIST**

This book is not meant to be used, nor should it be used to diagnose or treat any medical condition. For diagnosis or treatment of any medical problem, consult your own physician. The publisher and author are not responsible for any specific health or allergy conditions that may require medical supervision and are not liable for any damages or negative consequences from any treatment, action, application or preparation, to any person reading or following the information in this book. References are provided for informational purposes only and do not endorse any websites or other sources. Readers should be aware that the websites listed in this book may change.

CONTENTS:

Chapter 1:

Things you need to know about The Keto

A brief history of the ketogenic diet

It is a known fact that the ketogenic diet has never been created intentionally. It appeared as a by-product of a treatment for epilepsy known as fasting. Back when epilepsy was still a mystery, and the treatment was still being tested, scientists discovered that the patients who fasted were able to minimize their seizures. Then Dr. Wilder explained how the fasting helped in this. He said patients who fasted forced their bodies to run on excess fats, which led to the production of ketones.

Patients who fasted were getting better, but the diet was unsustainable. So, Dr. Wilder came up with a new idea to make the body produce ketones without fasting: ketogenic diet.

The discovery of the ketogenic diet has set the stage for many other discoveries. Dr. Peterman was able to standardize the ketogenic diet, having developed this calculation:

- 1g of protein per kilogram of bodyweight

- 10-15g of carbohydrates

- The rest of the calories should be allocated to fats

What is the ketogenic diet?

Don't let the word confuse you. The ketogenic diet is quite simple. It means two things, actually. The first one is the low carbohydrates intake. And the second is the intake of more fats. A lot of people get the wrong idea; I've met a couple of people who actually think the keto diet is about eating a lot of either proteins or fats. No, it is not only about eating either fats or proteins, let's get this straight. The fats are essential and cannot be substituted with proteins. On the contrary, protein must not be consumed in large quantities.

The whole idea about the ketogenic diet is to consume more fat, some proteins, and minimum carbs. When your body gets used to taking in more fats and fewer carbs, it will become efficient in burning fat for energy.

This is possible through a process called ketosis. The liver converts fats to ketones.

The water and mineral balance in the body can also be affected by ketosis, so it is advisable to include more water salts and mineral supplements in your diet.

Burning fat for energy

When we consume carbs, our body breaks it down to glucose. A hormone called insulin pushes glucose into the bloodstream. Basically, glucose is a kind of fuel for the body.

The major source of energy for the body is glucose, which is accumulated only when there is a sufficient amount of carbs. But what happens when the body doesn't get any carbs? Do we feel a lack of energy then? This brings us back to our ketogenic diet.

When on a keto diet, the intake of carbs is very minimal, and so the body is forced to find an alternative source of energy to keep working.

This is where body fats come into play. The fatty acids in the liver are converted to ketone bodies, which are ketones. This is realized through a process known as ketosis. Ketones are now the new source of energy for the body. And such ketosis is the goal of the ketogenic diet.

Different types of ketones are produced when fatty acids break down. Let's name three of them:

• Acetoacetate (AcAc): produced during ketosis.

• Beta-hydroxybutyric acid (BHB): produced from acetoacetate.

• Acetone: formed simultaneously as a byproduct of acetoacetate.

Summary:

So basically, the ketogenic diet is just about eating more fats and the minimally possible amount of carbs. And the end goal is to produce more ketones from fatty acids.

Benefits of the ketogenic diet

Over the years, people have been quite reluctant to jump on a low-carb diet. They have always had the impression that a low-carb diet could lead to a high cholesterol level, which could further result in heart diseases.

But on the contrary, scientists have found that low-carb diets actually are not just dealing with epilepsy alone, but with many other health issues as well, such as weight loss, high blood pressure, and so on.

These numerous benefits of the ketogenic diet include:

1. The ketogenic diet reduces appetite:

When people turn to diets, one of their most significant challenges is usually hunger because the diet forbids them to eat what they usually eat.

This is why the majority of people never get to the end with their diet plans. But research has shown that the low-carb diet tends to reduce people's appetite and so they don't get hungry that often anymore. People who are on low-carb diets tend to consume fewer calories.

Summary:

Studies have shown that cutting down the intake of carbs can decrease appetite and the amount of calorie intake.

2. Low-carb diet helps in shedding excess weight:

Reducing your intake of carbohydrates makes your weight go down faster than reducing your fat intake. The fastest way to lose weight is by cutting down the intake of carbs.

This is becauselow-carb diets actively get rid of excess water in the body and reduce the insulin level in the body.

Research has shown that people on low-carb diets lose

about 2-3 times more weight than people on low-fat diets.

Summary:

Low-carb diets cause more short-termed weight loss than low-fat diets. The weight loss benefit of low-carb diets fades away with time (in the long term).

3. Loss of abdominal fat:

Not all the fat in our body is of the same kind. There are two types of fat: the subcutaneous fat and the visceral fat. The visceral fat is usuallyfound in the abdominal area. It is the primary reason for big bellies.

Research has shown that the significant fat loss during the low-carb diet takes place in the abdominal area. Abdominal fat could cause health problems.

So, the low-carb diet will save us from excessive harmful fat and health issues such as inflammations.

Summary:

Most of the fat loss during the ketogenic diet is the harmful abdominal fat, which usually causes a number of metabolic complications.

4. Significant drops in the amount of triglycerides:

There are fat molecules in our bloodstream known as triglycerides. It can cause serious heart problems. One of the causes of high fasting of triglycerides, especially in people who lead a sedentary way of life, is the intake of carbs.

When you can cut down carbs from your diet, you also prevent the appearance of blood triglycerides, which cause heart diseases.

Summary:

Low-carbohydrate diets efficiently reduce the blood triglycerides, which are heavy molecules that raise your risks of heart diseases.

5. Levels of "good" HDL (High-Density Lipoprotein) cholesterol increases:

There is good cholesterol HDL (high-density lipoprotein) and bad cholesterol, LDL (low-density lipoprotein). The bad cholesterol could lead to serious heart problems, and one of the ways to prevent that is to increase your good HDL. An increased HDL will reduce the risk of heart diseases.

Consumption of fats increases levels of HDL, which is good cholesterol.

Summary:

Low-carb diets are rich in fats, so they cause an impressive rise in the HDL level, which is good cholesterol.

6. Reduced blood sugar and insulin level:

Millions of people across the world are plagued with diabetes and insulin resistance. It's no secret that ketogenic diets help drastically with diabetes and insulin resistance.

A low-carb diet helps to reduce the blood sugar level and also increases insulin levels.

People on low-carb diets with diabetes may have to reduce their insulin dosage by about 50%. Some studies also showed that, in just about 6 months, 95% of people with diabetes (type 2) on a low-carb diet tend to reduce the daily intake of their glucose-lowering medication.

Summary:

When you reduce your carbs intake, you decrease your blood sugar and insulin levels, which could treat or maybe even cure type 2 diabetes.

7. Blood pressure normalization:

Heart diseases, kidney failures, and strokes are all caused by high blood pressure and hypertension. Ketogenic diets are known for reducing blood pressure, which in turn decreases your risk of strokes, kidney failures, and heart diseases.

Summary:

Your blood pressure significantly decreases when you exclude carbs from your diet. And that, in turn, prevents a lot of common diseases such as strokes and kidney failure.

8. Prevents metabolic syndrome:

Metabolic syndrome features several symptoms, such as:

• Abdominal obesity

• HDL, good cholesterol, is getting low

• Increased blood pressure

• Increased triglycerides

• Increased fasting blood sugar level

High risks of diabetes and heart diseases are also closely associated with metabolic syndrome.

However, a ketogenic diet can help to eliminate all the chances of having those syndromes.

Summary:

A healthy ketogenic diet can effectively reduce and reverse all the symptoms of metabolic syndrome.

9. LDL (Low-Density Lipoprotein), will improve:

Heart attacks are common for those with high LDL, bad cholesterol, levels.

We should, however, note that the sizes are very significant. When the molecules are small, the risks of a heart attack are higher, but when the molecules are bigger, the risks of a heart attack are reduced.

Low-carb diets increase the sizes of the molecules and make them lower in quantity, thereby reducing the risk of a heart attack for lots of people.

Summary:

The size of bad LDL molecules decreases significantly when you're on a low-carb diet, and it decreases their (bad LDL molecules) harmful effects. It could also lower the total number of bad LDL molecules in your bloodstream.

10. Treats brain disorder:

There is a part of our brain, which can only burn glucose.This is why, even in the absence of carbs, the liver still produces glucose from protein.

However, a large part of our brain uses ketones, which are formed when the carbs intake is low enough.

This mechanism can be used in treating epilepsy in children who do not respond to their medicine well. Over 50% of the children on the ketogenic diet had a high reduction of seizures. And over 16% were cured of seizures completely.

Ketogenic diets are also understudies for treating other brain conditions now.

Summary:

Low carbohydrate diets are the key to treating and curing epilepsy in children.

In conclusion:

We have been able to highlight the significant advantages of the ketogenic diet. All the benefits are easy to achieve. Just stay away from carbs and eat more fats.

Do you want to improve your health? Just follow the ketogenic diet!

Various types of ketogenic diets

The ketogenic diet has multiple types. They are:

• Standard ketogenic diet (SKD): this type of ketogenic diet means very high fat, moderate proteins, and low carbs diet. Here, 70 to 75% of your diet are fats, 20 to 25% of your diet are proteins, and the remaining 5% are carbs.

•High protein ketogenic diet: this basically means more proteins. The ratio for this is 60% of fats, 35% of protein, and 5% of carbs. The standard ketogenic diet is similar to this high protein diet, and the difference is that this has more protein in the diet.

•Cynical ketogenic diets (CKD): this kind of diet simply

means there will be days of high carbohydrates intake. For instance, seven days of the keto diet and three days of high carbs consumption.

•Targeted ketogenic diet (TKD): this diet is for people who work out, people like athletes. It allows you to consume some carbs around your workouts.

The standard ketonic diet and the high protein diet are the most widely used. They have been studied comprehensively and in-depth.

The targeted and cynical ketogenic diets are more advanced methods for those who do heavy workouts, such as bodybuilders and athletes.

Macronutrients, what are they?

FATS	PROTEIN	CARBS

Here are the primary macronutrients found in our foods and beverages:

•**Fats**

•Protein

•Carbohydrates

Usually, when someone who is on a ketogenic diet talks about macronutrients, he/she is referring to how fats, protein, and carbohydrates are broken down in their foods or diet.

Tip:

It can be quite challenging to keep tracking the intake of the macronutrients when starting the ketogenic diet.That's why people are generally advised to start with the carbs consumption around or under 20 grams for at least two weeks. To start it in an easy way, simply use the meal plans listed in this book.

Later, it will be easier to track the other macronutrients. Fats and protein, as well as the intake of calories. Tracking calories can help people who have problems with overeating.

What are the best macros on a ketogenic diet?

This chart is an excellent visual representation of how your ketogenic diet should look like:

KETO MACROS

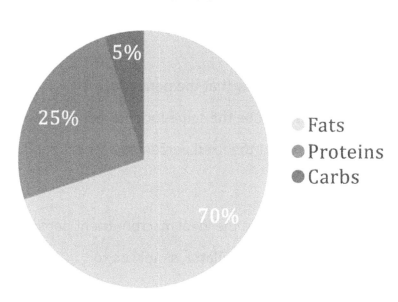

As we can see from the chart, the fat should take up the highest percentage of your calorie intake, which is about 70-75% of your overall calorie intake.

The protein intake should be moderate, just about 20-25% of your calorie intake.

And finally, your carbohydrates intake should be minimal. They should take up just 5% of your calorie intake (20-25 grams of pure carbs a day).

It is important to know that the percentage of macronutrients can't be the same for each person. The diagram above is not the fixed percentage allocation for everyone.

You can also calculate the ideal macronutrient percentage for you with the keto calculator, simply go to www.ruled.me/keto-calculator/.

The macros calculator is great to start with. However, please note that you may need to adjust the percentage of macros to achieve the desired results.

Chapter 2:

Nutritional ketosis

What does nutritional ketosis mean?

RAPID WEIGHT LOSS   SUSTAINED FAT LOSS   REDUCED CRAVINGS   STABLE ENERGY   CLEAR COGNITION

Ketosis is also called nutritional ketosis. It is a metabolic state that makes the body use up fat and to produce ketones (ketone bodies) of about 0.5 to 5 millimoles per each liter of the blood.

Most standard American diets are high-carb diets. When the body consumes carbohydrates (such as starches and sugar), it breaks them down into glucose (also known as simple sugar) during digestion. This glucose goes into the bloodstream. When this happens, the blood glucose level rises, and this causes the pancreas to release a hormone known as insulin. This hormone, insulin, regulates the blood sugar level, and enables the glucose in the blood to enter the cells, be absorbed and used for energy. There usually is an excess of glucose left in the body, and it is stored in the liver and muscles. This reserve is called glycogen or glycogen stores.

The opposite happens on a ketogenic diet. Your intake of fats is high, the protein is moderate, and the carbohydrates are minimal.

This reduces the likeliness of the glucose and insulin release in your body. Consequently, your glucose level drops, and the glycogen stores in your body will also be depleted. The fatty acids will then be released, converted to ketones and used for energy.

How to get into ketosis

There are seven important things you need to do to reach your ketosis:

LIMIT CARBOHYDRATES: your carbohydrate intake should be limited to at most 20 grams per day. A keto diet is a strict low-carb diet.

You don't have to limit fiber too; it actually helps to reach ketosis.

Keto meal plans and recipes in this book are designed to keep your carbs intake under 20 grams per day without having to count.

EAT ENOUGH FAT: the ketogenic diet is a low-carb diet, so you also need to eat enough fat to get energy. If you're someone who loves to eat, then eat properly, only this time eat a lot of fats. That's the main difference between the ketogenic diet and fasting. Fasting is not sustainable; you get hungry, weak and tired. So, if you find yourself always getting hungry, eat more fats, add more (olive) oil or butter, etc. to your food. It helps to speed up ketosis as your body converts more fats into ketones.

EAT PROTEIN MODERATELY: do not make the mistake of eating lots of protein. It slows down ketosis because an excess of protein converts into glucose.

Try to keep protein at a minimal level of 1.5 grams per day per kilogram of body weight that would be equal to 100 grams of protein for a person who weighs around 70 kilos (154 lbs).Keto is not a high-protein diet. We should consume the amount of protein our body needs but no more.

SLEEP ENOUGH: On average, a person sleeps for not less than 7 hours. And it's well to keep stress under control by resting well.

People who don't sleep well make their bodies and minds stressed. When you don't sleep enough, you get stressed, and it causes your blood sugar to rising, which slows down ketosis.

And it's even harder to stay on a diet when stressed because it becomes more difficult to resist the temptations of wanting to eat. Sleeping well and controlling stress on its own doesn't initiate ketosis, but at least it helps to boost ketosis.

ADDING EXERCISE: exercising while on a low-carb diet usually helps to increase the production of ketone bodies.

It also helps to lose weight faster as well as reversing type 2 diabetes.

STOP SNACKING: Don't eat when you aren't even hungry

simply because there's food around. Doing that can boost ketosis and weight loss.

If you can't avoid snacking, do it when you are hungry and do it with a ketogenic snack, it will decrease the damage.

ADDITION OF INTERMITTENT FASTING: you'll need to skip breakfast and only eat during 8 hours of the day, fasting for the next 16 hours. This kind of fasting is very effective in boosting ketone levels, weight loss, and reverses type 2 diabetes.

It is usually easier to do on keto.

Chapter 3:

The keto side effects

The keto flu and how to make things go right

There are several symptoms of the keto side effects, also called the keto flu. They include:

- Irritability

- Dizziness

- Fatigue

- Nausea

- Headaches

- Difficulties in focusing ("brain fog")

- Absence of motivation

- Muscle cramps

•Sugar cravings

What causes the keto flu?

The transition from burning sugar for energy to burning fat for energy is what causes the keto flu.

During keto, the body is starving of glucose and so the insulin level drops. The reduction of insulin is actually very healthy, and it causes ketosis. Once the insulin has dropped, the liver begins to convert fats to ketones.Ketones are absorbed by the cells instead of glucose and used for energy. The state in which your body uses ketones for energy is called ketosis.

However, the brain and other organs would need time to adjust to the new source of energy (ketones). Your body will react to the changes by releasing more sodium into urine, along with water. This is why, at the beginning of ketosis, some people urinate a bit more often than before.

These changes often cause a rapid weight loss. However, losing too much sodium and water is also the reason for symptoms of the keto flu.

The way the body reacts to the keto transition is very individual. Some might feel a bit tired during the first couple of days on keto. Others may experience symptoms that could severely affect their ability to function for several days.

You need to know that the keto flu won't be unbearable for anyone if the proper steps are taken to deal with the symptoms.

How to cure the keto flu

Simple way to fight keto flu with food. Check the symptoms listed below and fix them adding sodium, magnesium or potassium.

Headache, brain fog, fatigue, muscle cramps

Fix: sodium

Himalayan salt, bacon, bouillon, salted nuts

Muscle weakness, muscle cramps, anxiety

Fix: magnesium

Dark chocolate, almonds, spinach, avocados

Low blood pressure, cramping, constipation, muscle weakness

Fix: potassium

Salmon, avocados, dark leafy greens, mushrooms

Even though most of the symptoms of the keto flu are short-termed, there is still no need to endure pain even if it's for a short period of time, especially when you can treat them and feel yourself well again! The most important step, (and usually the only step needed) is the first step:

INCREASE YOUR SALT AND WATER INTAKE (MOST IMPORTANT STEP): The loss of salt and water is what causes most of the keto flu symptoms. In order to remedy and reverse the symptoms, you need to consume more salt and water, which will normalize the water balance of your body.

During the early stages of your keto, you might experience lethargy, headaches, dizziness, nausea, etc. A simple way to treat this is to take a glass of water with half a teaspoon of salt stirred into it. This can alleviate your keto flu symptoms within 15 to 30 minutes. You can repeat this twice or more during a day, depending on how often you feel the symptoms.

A fine alternative to water with salt can be chicken broth, beef stock, meat broth, bouillon, bone broth, and consommé. You can also stir in salted butter if you like.

If you use low-sodium bone broth, you can simply add one or two pinches of salt to it.

It is important to drink enough water. The higher your weight is, the more water you lose, and the more water you should take to replace the water you've lost. When on a keto diet, you should drink up to 3 liters of water per day. This doesn't mean that the 3 liters of water are an addition to other drinks. Beverages and teas also help to increase body fluid.

People normally experience constipation during the early stages of keto too. Water, electrolytes, and sodium help to eliminate constipation.

ADDITIONAL FAT: sometimes, you can keep feeling the

keto flu symptoms even after increasing the intake of sodium and water. If this happens, increase your intake of fat.

Most new low-carb dieters are usually reluctant to take more fat because of the false information which has been spreading for years about fat being unhealthy. When you drastically reduce your intake of carbs without increasing your consumption of fat, your body will assume you're starving. As we know, starvation leads a person to be tired, weak, and unhappy. A proper keto diet contains enough fats, so after a meal, you can work for hours without eating and still have lots of energy. At the onset of your keto diet, you are encouraged to eat lots of fat until your body adjusts to using ketones and fats as its main source of energy.

Once your body adapts, you can use your appetite as a guide to cut down on excess fats while making sure you keep a balance between satiety and hunger.

In fact, if you are unsure about this, eat more fat. Our keto recipes also have enough fats in relation to protein and carbs.

SLOWER TRANSITION: Sometimes, even after increasing

water, salt, and fats intake, you keep feeling the keto flu symptoms. At this point, I suggest you wait a few more days. Health benefits of the ketogenic diet are really worth hanging on.For instance, it reverses type 2 diabetes and is best for weight loss. The symptoms would definitely go once you become a fat burner.

If, however, you cannot endure these symptoms, then you can slow down the transition to ketoby eating more carbs. You could increase your carbs intake to about 20-50 grams per day. It is called a moderate-carb diet.

This would, however, slow down the ketosis and inhibit rapid and drastic health improvements, but it's still healthier, especially if the carbs you are cutting off are processed foods and sugar. And the keto flu wouldn't be a problem anymore.

Once your body gets used to moderate carbs, you can continue taking less than 20 grams of carbs per day and see how your body responds. You can see whether it prefers moderate or low-carb diets.

PHYSICAL ACTIVITY SHOULD BE MODERATE: Doing too much exercise may elevate the keto flu symptoms.

Dr. Steve Phinney, a renowned ketogenic researcher, conducted a study on the endurance capacity of athletes and obese people on a keto diet, the results proved that their strength reduced within the early stages of keto. However, by the fourth week of their keto diet, their physical performance had improved way better than before they started the keto diet.

It's fine to do mind-body exercises, gentle yoga, stretches and even walking when starting keto. It can even make you feel better. But strenuous exercises should be avoided to prevent any additional burden to the stress your body already feels due to adjustments to a new source of energy.

Take it easy during the early stages of the keto, and then you can slowly increase the intensity of your exercise step by step.

DO NOT RESTRICT FOOD INTAKE: Naturally, some people eat less during the beginning of keto basically because the appetite for fatty foods is low, so they might feel nauseous at having to eat majorly fats.

But others could get very hungry. So they cut down on their

eating because they feel they are taking in way too many calories, which could deter the weight loss they want to achieve. The first phase of the keto is induction. This stage is about maximum fat burning and a speedy achieving of the state of ketosis in the body is expected. It is a very tough phase. At this stage, you are permitted to eat as much food, which helps fuel your body, as long as you keep your net carbs under 20 grams.

It is not recommended to worry about your calorie intake or macronutrients. Staying hungry or worrying about how much you're eating might actually worsen the keto flu symptoms.

You are advised to eat well. After your body got used to ketosis, you would become less hungry and your appetite would drop.

Eat the needed amount of the keto foods when you're hungry, and if you want to snack, turn to a keto snack such as boiled egg. Do not overeat, eat till you are no longer hungry and not till you feel bloated or heavy, do that by paying attention to fullness and hunger signals.

Chapter 4:

How to switch to keto. To do and to eat lists

Five steps to switch to keto

1. THE PANTRY SHOULD BE CLEARED:

When starting keto, the first and most important step is to get rid of temptations. Go to your pantry and throw out all food not needed for keto.

If you are living with someone, let them know what you want to throw away from the refrigerator and why, if it's something that they cannot get rid of, then kindly ask them to keep it out of your sight to avoid temptations.

Grains and Starches: It is imperative to start by getting rid of foods like rice, cereals, pasta, macaroni, bagels, wraps, and bread. Everything starch-based needs to be thrown away as keto doesn't need them as a source of energy at all.

Foods Containing Sugar: Although this might be difficult for a lot of us, we need to remove all refined sugars from our kitchen too. This ranges from drinks, juice, milk, and desserts like cakes, ice cream, and chocolate.

Legumes: This is probably confusing to someone, but the fact is legumes contain a lot of carbs which we would not need on our ketogenic diet. So, it is necessary to remove all lentils, peas, and even beans from our kitchens too.

Processed oils and fats: Yes, there are a lot of oils that are recommended for keto diets, such as avocado oil, olive oil, and coconut oil.

However, there are also a lot of oils that are not keto-friendly, for example, sunflower oil, vegetable oil, canola oil, soya beans oil, and corn oil. We need to get rid of these oils.

Fruits: You don't need to stay off fruits, after all some are actually very keto-friendly and serve as good snacks. However, there are some full carb fruits that you need to stay away from, such as apples, grapes, bananas, mangoes, and dates. Dried fruits should be removed from your diet too, most of them contain unwelcomed sugar.

2. THE PANTRY SHOULD BE FILLED UP:

Since you are removing all the non-keto friendly foods, we need to fill up the pantry with keto foods.

Essential requirements:

Some basic foods can always be easily used to cook a keto meal. They include:

•Coffee and tea

•Condiments (pesto, sriracha, mayonnaise, and mustard)

•Nuts and seeds

•Spices and herbs

•Lemon juice

•Broths (chicken, beef and bone)

Meats: any kind of meat can be used for your keto diet. Use what you like the most. It can be beef, lamb, pork, and chicken. If you have extra cash, it is advised to buy organic or grass-fed meats. Fish is also not bad, but try to consume fish that are caught in the natural water bodies and not fish that are farmed. Finally, eggs are very keto-friendly.

Vegetables: some of the keto-friendly vegetables are mushrooms, Brussel sprouts, broccoli and asparagus, bell pepper, tomatoes, onions, most green vegetables.

Fruits: Although we have excluded a lot of your favorite fruits as not keto-friendly, some are great when on keto. Feel free to snack on small quantities of berries such as strawberries, raspberries, and mulberries. You can also eat oranges and grapefruits. Lemon juice is also a good keto-friendly sweetener.

Dairy: Dairy contains high amounts of fats and, therefore, it is highly keto-friendly. However, dairy products like yogurts and milk are not recommended for your keto because of the large amount of sugar contained in them.

Oils and fats: We've already discussed this in the previous sections: oils such as avocado, olive, and coconut are keto-friendly. You can also use butter and bacon fat as the basis of your meals. It's even better to cook meat and vegetables.

3. EQUIP YOUR KITCHEN

We've listed several kitchen essentials which would ensure that you are ready and able to make any meal that the keto diet offers us. Almost all of our keto recipes are very simple and straightforward, and if your kitchen is well equipped, your cooking should be fun and effortless.

Food scale: this is one of the most important kitchen equipment to have in your kitchen. It helps you to measure your foods to ensure you are not overestimating your cooking. It also helps you track your calorie intake as you can measure the grams of whatever you are eating, this helps you track your progress easily.

Food processors: this is very helpful kitchen equipment. It helps you blend any food you want; it makes preparing smoothies, salsas, and sauces a lot easier and faster.

Spiralizer: spiralizer is the next kitchen equipment on the list. The spiralizer is good for making noodles out of vegetables. Since pasta and noodles have been cut off from your foods, you can eat noodles made from vegetables. The most common vegetable noodles are zucchini and zoodle noodles. And they are great substitutions for regular noodles and pasta.

Cast iron pans: the last item on the list is cast iron pans.

Normal pans are fine too, but the cast iron pan is recommended for several reasons. Firstly, they retain heat well. Secondly, they can be used on the stove and in the oven. Thirdly, they're healthier and safer to use because no chemical additives are added to them when they are manufactured.

4. PLAN YOUR MEAL

It's not enough to have all the kitchen equipment and new ingredients. We also need to know how to use them properly. The best way to do this is to follow the instructions about a meal plan from professionals in the field. Some of us may want to adjust our meal plan to suit our preferences without going beyond what is allowed, at least for the first few weeks of your keto diet, stick strictly to your meal plans. At least stick to them until you're sure of how much calories should be going into your body.

Once you're familiar with everything, you can change the meal plan to suit your liking, restricting yourself to what you've learned about the keto diet.

5. EXERCISE

After you're off and well into your keto diet, you would experience some weight loss, and it is imperative to exercise to keep the body active and healthy. You should exercise more, but it varies for individuals.

If you had never exercised before starting keto, then do not engage in any strenuous workout. Start with light exercises such as jogging two or three times a week. But if you have worked out before keto, then you should increase your workouts. Don't just start doing strenuous exercises, rather increase your workouts bit by bit. There is a need for a gradual increase so that your body can adapt to any changes that might occur.

Once your body gets comfortable with the new source of energy, ensure to give the stock a try. During those high-intensity days, the stock can help you work out longer, harder, and recover faster.

It can boost your keto diet when you need it.

Foods to eat

The majority of your meals should be based around these

foods:

•CREAM AND BUTTER: if possible, look for grass-fed.

•SEEDS AND NUTS: flax seeds, pumpkin seeds, chia seeds, walnuts, almonds, etc.

•LOW-CARB VEGETABLES: bell pepper, tomatoes, onions, most green vegetables, etc.

•FATTY FISH: fish like mackerel, tuna, salmon, and trout.

•MEAT: bacon, turkey, ham, steak, red meat, chicken, and sausages.

•EGGS: go for omega-3 whole eggs or pastured eggs.

•CHEESE: opt for unprocessed cheese, such as blue, mozzarella, cheddar, goat, and cream.

•HEALTHY OILS: avocado oil, coconut oil, and majorly extra virgin olive oil.

•FRUITS: oranges, mulberries, grapefruits, strawberries, raspberries, lemons, apricots, kiwis.

•AVOCADO: guacamole (freshly made) and whole avocados.

•CONDIMENTS: different healthy herbs, one can use salt, spices, and pepper.

Basing your diet primarily on single-ingredient foods is best.

Foods to avoid

Basically, all high-carb foods should be restricted.

These are some of the foods to steer clear of on the ketogenic diet:

•Unhealthy fats: restrict your consumption of mayonnaise, and oils are gotten from vegetables.

•Diet or low-fat products: they are generally high in carbohydrates and extremely processed.

•Sugar-free diet foods: foods like these are normally highly processed. These are normally high in alcohol with sugar and can decrease the ketones level.

•Some sauces and condiments: they normally have unnatural fats and sugar.

•Tubers and root vegetables: carrots, potatoes, parsnips,

sweet potatoes, and so on.

•Starches or grains: pasta, rice, cereal, products from wheat, and so on.

•Legumes or beans: lentils, peas, chickpeas, kidney beans, and so on.

•Alcohol: most alcohols can inhibit ketosis in your body due to their carbohydrate level. But if you wish some, choose a low carb beverages such as: dry wine, dry martini, whiskey, brandy, tequila, vodka.

Summary:

Stay away from high-carb foods like rice, cereals, legumes, grains, sugar, juice, candies, and the majority of fruits.

A list of 44 low-carbohydrate foods

Meats and eggs

The various kinds of meats and eggs are all almost zero carbs. However, the liver, organ meat, is an exception because it contains around 5% (13) carbs.

BEEF (ZERO)

A lot of vital nutrients can be found in beef, such as vitamin B12 and iron. It is also very satisfying. There are so many kinds of beef products, ranging from hamburgers to ribeye steak to ground beef.

Carbs: Zero

PORK, BACON INCLUDED (USUALLY ZERO):

Pork is one of the delicious kind of meats, so low-carb dieters normally prefer bacon.

It is usually allowed to consume bacon on a keto (low-carb) diet even though it is not healthy due to the fact that it is processed meat.

Make sure your bacon is bought locally, without any non-natural components. And also avoid burning the pork while cooking it.

Carbs: usually zero but always check the label to be sure it is not bacon treated with sugar.

EGGS (ALMOST ZERO):

One of the healthy and most nutritious food is an egg.

Various nutrients are packed in them. Some of these nutrients are compounds that improve eye health, and some are nutrients that are important for your brain health.

Carbs: Almost Zero

CHICKEN (ZERO):

One of the world's most well-known meat is chicken. It's a great source of protein and rich in many valuable nutrients.

The fatty parts of the chicken, like the wings and thighs, are preferable for people on a ketogenic diet.

Carbs: zero (0).

LAMB (ZERO):

Like beef, lambs contain many useful nutrients. These nutrients include vitamin B12 and iron. A lamb is often grass-fed, and its meat is usually rich in useful fatty acids and linoleic acid.

Carbs: zero (0).

MEAT JERKY (USUALLY ZERO):

Meat jerky is a type of meat that is usually cut in strips and then dried.

Jerky could be a perfect snack for low-carb diets as long as it doesn't have any artificial condiments or sugar.

Nevertheless, it is better to prepare it by yourselves because most of the jerky meat sold in stores is not healthy due to being highly processed.

Carbs: it varies depending on the type if its jerky with simple seasoning, then the carbs should be relatively zero.

Other kinds of low-carb meats:

Venison, bison, veal, turkey

Seafood

Seafood (fish and others) are usually very healthy and extremely nutritious.

B12, omega-3 fatty acids and iodine can specifically be richly found in seafood. They are nutrients that people don't usually get sufficient quantities.

Just like meat, virtually all seafood has little to zero carbs in them.

SHELLFISH (4-5% OF CARBOHYDRATES):

One of the world's most nutritious food is shellfish. Everybody should really try to include shellfish into their daily meal menus.

They are almost of the same level as organ meats in relation to their amount of nutrients. And they are also low-carb foods.

Carbs: 4-5 g of carbohydrates for every 100 g of shellfish.

SARDINES (ZERO):

Sardines are one of the foods with the richest composition of nutrients. It contains almost all the nutrients our body needs.

It is an oily fish. People normally eat the whole fish, together with the bones.

Carbs: zero (0).

SALMON (ZERO):

Salmon is packed with iodine, B12, and a sufficient quantity of vitamin D3.

Salmon is well-known by a health-conscious person for good reasons.

It is a fish which has substantial quantities of heart-healthy fats, that is because it is a fatty fish. The heart-healthy fats that it contains are known as omega-3 fatty acids.

Carbs: zero (0).

TROUTS (ZERO):

Just like salmon, trout is a kind of fatty fish that contains a lot of significant nutrients and also omega-3 fatty acids.

Carbs: zero (0).

Other kinds of low-carb seafood and fish:

Catfish, cord, haddock, shrimp, halibut, lobster, herring, tuna

Vegetables

Most of the vegetables we know contain low quantities of carbs. Cruciferous veggies and green leafy veggies have very low amounts of carbs. Most of the carbs contain fibers.

In contrast, vegetables with starchy roots such as potatoes and sweet potatoes contain large amounts of carbs.

CAULIFLOWER (5%):

Cauliflower can be used to cook different meals in your kitchen. They are quite multipurpose and scrumptious.

It is rich in folate, vitamin C, and vitamin K.

Carbs: 5g for every 100g, also 5g for each cup.

KALE (10%):

Kale offers several health benefits. It is a very well-known vegetable among health-conscious individuals.

It is packed with vitamin K, carotene antioxidants, vitamin C and also fiber.

Carbs: 10g for every 100g, also 7g for each cup.

ASPARAGUS (2%):

Asparagus is a spring vegetable that is extremely nutritious.

It is very rich in carotene antioxidants, vitamin K, vitamin C, folate, and fibers.

Likened to other vegetables, it is relatively very high in protein.

Carbs: 3 grams for every cup, 2 grams for every 100 grams.

MUSHROOMS:

Though they are theoretically not plants, the edible ones are regarded as vegetables.

They possess sufficient quantities of potassium and are rich in vitamin B.

Carbs: 3 grams for every 100 grams, also 3 grams for every cup.

GREEN BEANS (7%):

Green beans are normally consumed in a manner similar to vegetables even though they are theoretically legumes.

They are tremendously rich in vitamin C, protein, Vitamin K, potassium, magnesium, fiber, and many other nutrients.

Carbs: 8 grams for each cup, or 7 grams for every 100 grams.

BROCCOLI (7%):

Broccoli is a cruciferous vegetable that can be consumed both raw and cooked. It is very tasty.

It is rich in vitamin K, powerful cancer-fighting plant compounds, vitamin C, and fibers.

Carbs: 6 grams for each cup, 7 grams for every 100 grams.

BRUSSELS SPROUTS (7%):

Brussels sprouts are related to broccoli and kale. They are very nourishing and rich in vitamins K and C, also possessing various advantageous plant compounds.

Carbs: 6 grams for each half cup, and 7 grams for every 100 grams.

EGGPLANTS (6%):

Another fruit that is frequently eaten as a vegetable is eggplant.

It is very rich in fiber and has a lot of fascinating uses.

Carbs: 6 grams for each cup, 7 grams for every 100 grams.

BELL PEPPER (6%):

Bell pepper is a vegetable/fruit with a pleasant and distinct flavor.

Bell peppers are very rich in nutrients like vitamin C, carotene antioxidants, and fibers.

Carbs: 9 grams for each cup, and 6 grams for every 100 grams.

CUCUMBER (9%):

Cucumbers are well-known vegetables. They have a mild flavor. They have low quantities of vitamin K and consist mainly of water.

Carbs: 2 grams for each half cup, or 4 grams for every 100 grams.

ONIONS (9%):

Onions add the tastiest flavor to your recipes. They are one of the tastiest plants on planet Earth.

They possess a lot of antioxidants, anti-inflammatory compounds, and fibers.

Carbs: 11 grams for each cup, or 9 grams for every 100 grams.

TOMATOES (4%):

Tomatoes are usually eaten as vegetables, even though they are actually berries or fruits.

They are rich in potassium and vitamin C.

Carbs: 7 grams for each large tomato, and 4 grams for every 100 grams.

Other low-carb vegetables:

Swiss chard, cabbage, celery, spinach, zucchini

You can consume lots of vegetables without exceeding your carbohydrate limit because almost all vegetables are low in carbohydrates with the exception of vegetables with starchy roots.

Fruits

In general, fruits are considered as healthy. However, they are very controversial among low-carb dieters.

Unlike vegetables, fruits are not as keto-friendly because a lot of them are packed with carbs.

If you are advised to take fruits while on a keto diet, try to limit your intake to 1 or 2 fruits depending on your carb intake limit. However, fruits with high-fat contents, such as olives and avocado, are not excluded from your foods to eat. Another exceptional choice is low-sugar berries.

AVOCADO (8.5%):

In addition to being high in carbs, it is rich in fats. Avocado is quite a unique fruit.

Avocado has sufficient quantities of various nutrients. It is especially rich in potassium and fibers.

Having seen the stated carb amounts below, remember that most of the carbs or at least 78% of the carbs are fibers. They have no digestible net carbohydrates.

Carbs: 13 grams per cup, 8.5 grams per 100 grams.

OLIVES (6%):

The olive is very rich in copper and iron, and it possesses a sufficient quantity of vitamin E. It is a tasty fruit that is rich in fats.

Carbs: 2 grams per ounce, and 6 grams per 100 grams.

GRAPEFRUITS (11%):

Grapefruit is a citrus fruit that belongs to the same plant family as oranges. They are greatly rich in carotene antioxidants and vitamin C.

Carbs: 13 grams per half a grapefruit, and 11 grams per 100 grams.

STRAWBERRIES (8%):

One of the most nutrient-condensed and low-carbohydrate fruits you could ever eat is strawberry. Strawberries are very rich in different antioxidants, vitamin C, and manganese.

Carbs: 11 grams per cup, and 8 grams per 100 grams.

APRICOT (11%):

A small amount of carbohydrates, plenty of potassium, and vitamin C can be found in every apricot. Apricots are very delicious fruits.

Carbs: 8 grams in two apricots, and 11 grams per 100

grams.

Other kinds of low-carb fruits:

Oranges, raspberries, lemon, mulberries, kiwis

Seeds and nuts

Seeds and nuts are normally rich in different macronutrients, including fibers, fats, and proteins, but low in carbs. They are well-known among low-carb dieters.

Seeds are often used for adding a crunch to our recipes and salads, while nuts are normally consumed as snacks.

Also, some baked foods and low-carbohydrate bread are normally made with flaxseed meal, almond flour, coconut flour, and other seeds and nuts flours.

ALMONDS (22%)

One of the world's best sources of magnesium is almond. Almonds are packed with vitamin E and fiber, and that is what most people hardly have sufficient amounts of.

They are very crunchy and tasty.

Almonds have also been proven to speed up weight loss. They are also very nourishing.

Carbs: 6 grams per ounce, and 22 grams per 100 grams.

CHIA SEEDS (44%):

Currently, one of the world's most popular health food is chia seeds.

Chia seeds are also among the richest sources of dietary fibers on earth.

They can be used for low-carbohydrates friendly food recipes. They are also packed with several vital nutrients.

Having seen the carbs numbers stated below, remember that 86% of the carbs are fibers. They possess very little consumable net carbs.

Carbs: 12 grams per ounce, otherwise 44 grams per 100 grams.

WALNUTS (14%):

Walnut is a delicious category of nut.

It is very rich in omega-3 fatty acids and alpha-linoleic acid

(ALA). It also possesses other types of nutrients.

Carbs: 4 grams per ounce, or 14 grams per 100 grams.

PEANUTS (16%):

Peanuts are normally made and eaten as if they are nuts, but they are actually legumes.

They are extremely rich in many vital vitamins and minerals, including magnesium, vitamin E, and fiber.

Carbs: 5 grams per ounce, or 16 grams per 100 grams.

Other low-carb seeds and nuts:

Pumpkin seeds, cashews, coconuts, flaxseeds, sunflower seeds, pistachios, macadamia nuts, hazelnuts

Dairy

If you like to consume dairy, then full-fat dairy is perfect for low-carb dieters. Still, do not forget to check the label to ensure there is no sugar in it.

FULL-FAT YOGURT (5%):

Full-fat yogurt has several similar nutrients as whole milk.

It's is outstandingly nourishing.

It is also packed with valuable probiotic bacteria due to its living cultures.

Carbs: 11 grams for each 8-ounce container, 5 grams for every 100 grams.

HEAVY CREAM (3%):

Heavy cream is an extremely rich dairy fat. It has a small amount of protein and limited carbs.

Low-carb dieters normally make use of heavy cream in their recipes and add it to their coffee. Low-carb dieters can make some kind of whipped dessert with a bowl of berries.

Carbs: 1 gram for each ounce, and 3 grams for every 100 grams.

CHEESE (1.3%):

Cheese can be consumed as a condiment in different tasty, delicious recipes and also eaten raw. Putting cheese on top of a bunless burger shows us that cheese goes well with meat. It is also one of the yummiest low-carb meals.

The quantity of nutrients in one fat slice of cheese equals the number of nutrients in a whole glass of milk.

Carbs: 0.4 grams for each slice of cheese, or 1.3 grams for every 100 grams of cheddar.

GREEK YOGURT (4%):

Unlike regular yogurt, Greek yogurt is a very thick yogurt. So many valuable nutrients, specifically protein, can be found in the Greek yogurt.

Carbs: 6 grams per 6-ounce contain, or 4 grams per 100 grams.

Oils and fats

Stay away from vegetable oils that are refined, such as corn oil and soya bean oil, because they are very unhealthy, especially when taken in large amounts.

However, there are other healthy oils that are great for keto dieters.

BUTTER (ZERO):

There was a time when butter was unpleased because of its

rich quantities of fats. However, it is regarded completely different today.

Grass-fed butter is rich in specific nutrients, hence, opt for it.

Carbs: Zero (0).

COCONUT OIL (ZERO):

Coconut oil is an extremely nourishing fat, loaded with medium-chain fatty acids that have a strong valuable effect on our metabolism.

The fatty acids are known to increase the burning of fat, aid loss of belly fat in people, and decrease appetite.

Carbs: Zero (0).

EXTRA VIRGIN OLIVE OIL (ZERO):

One of the most nourishing fats on earth is the extra virgin olive oil.

It is an important element of the keto diet and is packed with anti-inflammatory compounds and strong antioxidants.

Carbs: zero (0).

Other low-carb oils and fats:

Lard, tallow, avocado

Beverages

Beverages are tolerable to low-carb dieters as long as the beverage is sugar-free.

Remember to avoid juices made from fruits, because they have a high carb and sugar content.

TEA (ZERO):

Tea has numerous remarkable health advantages, especially green tea.

It can even fairly speed up the burning of fat.

Carbs: zero.

COFFEE (ZERO):

Coffee was once avoided like the plague; however, people have realized that coffee has one of the best dietary antioxidants and is also really nourishing.

Most of the people that have a little risk of severe diseases like Parkinson's disease, type 2 diabetes, and Alzheimer, and tend to live longer, in general, have been identified as coffee drinkers.

Ensure to add nothing unhealthy to your coffee; black coffee is preferable unless you're adding heavy cream or full-fat milk.

Carbs: zero (0).

CARBONATED SODA/CLUB SODA (ZERO):

When you add carbon dioxide and water together, it becomes a club soda. It is allowed as long as there is no sugar in it. Always check it on the label.

Carbs: zero (0).

WATER (ZERO):

Regardless of how your diet looks, water should be your default drink.

Carbs: Zero (0).

Other foods

Finally, there are foods that don't fit in any category. They include:

DARK CHOCOLATE:

Another low-carb snack is dark chocolate.

Make sure that it doesn't have any sugar, opt for real dark chocolate with 70-85% of cocoa.

It helps better blood pressure and brain capabilities.

25% of carbs in dark chocolate are mainly fibers.

Carbs: 13 grams for each- ounce piece, or 46 grams for every 100 grams.

SPICES, CONDIMENTS, AND HERBS:

There are so many tasty condiments, spices, and herbs. Almost all of them are very nutritional, improve the flavor of our dishes and have low quantities of carbs.

Ginger, pepper, garlic, salt, etc. are all good examples.

An easy low-carb shopping list

The shop corners are usually where these foods are commonly found, so it's a good guideline to buy there.

Your diet turns out to be much healthier than the standard Western diet when you consume more whole foods.

Even though the grass-fed and organic foods are very expensive, they are regarded as healthier options.

Make sure you opt for the lesser processed foods which are within your financial capacity.

•Cheese

•Coconut oil

- Olives

- Meat (pork, bacon, chicken, beef, lamb)

- Condiments (mustard, pepper, sea salt, garlic, and so on)

- Yogurt (no sugar or sweetener, full-fat)

- Olive oil

- Vegetables that are fresh (onions, peppers, greens, and so on)

- Lard

- Eggs (pastured egg and omega-3 enriched eggs should be chosen if available)

- Frozen vegetables (different mixtures, broccoli)

- Nuts

- Sour cream

- Blueberries (frozen or fresh)

- Butter

- Fish (salmon is preferable because it is fatty)

Chapter 5:

Keto recipes

Breakfasts

Keto breakfast sandwich (no-bread)

This delicious sandwich will certainly contribute to your best keto breakfast. A scrumptious piece of cheese is mixed with sizzling ham and eggs to form a no-bread sandwich.

Servings: 2

Ingredients:

- 2 tablespoon butter

- 4 eggs

- 1 oz. smoked deli ham

- 2 oz. cheddar cheese or provolone cheese or Edam cheese in thick slices

- pepper and salt

- Worcestershire sauce or Tabasco sauce

Cooking instructions:

1. Preheat your frying pan on a medium heat before adding butter. Then add eggs and let them fry on both sides. Add pepper and salt to taste.

2. Each egg forms the base and top of the sandwich. Start with the base. Place pastrami/ham/cold cuts on it. Put cheese on top and finish sandwiches with fried eggs. Leave the sandwiches in the pan over low heat so that the cheese would melt.

3. Add some Tabasco or Worcestershire sauce for a richer flavor. Serve while they are hot.

Advice:

Ham can be perfectly matched with French Dijon mustard.

An alternative to ham is fried bacon, or you may not use such type of ingredient at all. This sandwich can be served with avocado or green salad.

Carbs: 2g, Fat: 30g, Protein: 20g, Calories: 354 kcal

Quick and easy cream cheese pancakes

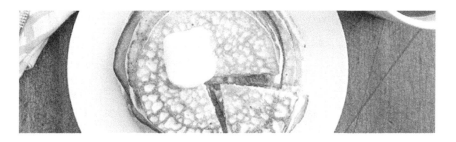

Servings: 2 (6 pancakes)

Ingredients:

• 4 oz softened cream cheese

• 4 eggs

• 2 teaspoon monk fruit or stevia sweetener

• ½ tsp vanilla extract

• 1 tablespoon butter (used for greasing the pan)

Cooking instructions:

1. Blend cream cheese, eggs, vanilla extract, and sweetener using a high-speed blender until the consistency of the mixture is uniform.

2. Preheat a frying pan or a large nonstick skillet over

medium heat, then melt ¼ teaspoon of butter in it.

3.   Pour ¼ cup of batter on the pan. Cover and let it cook for two minutes on both sides until it is golden brown. Repeat for the rest of the batter.

4.   Top up with butter, coconut butter, sugar-free maple syrup, or any other.

Carbs: 3g, Fat: 33g, Protein: 18g, Calories: 393 kcal

Blueberry pancakes

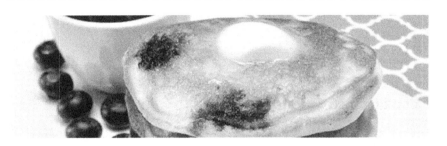

These delicious ketogenic blueberry pancakes are fast and simple to cook. Your perfect breakfast or brunch. Serve with whipped cream and let the whole family enjoy it!

Servings: 4

Ingredients:

- 6 eggs

- 4 oz. cream cheese

- 2/3 cup almond flour

- 3 oz. melted butter

- 2 tsp baking powder

- 2/3 cup oat fiber

- ½ lemon zest

- 1 pinch salt (optional)

- 3 oz. fresh blueberries

Cooking instructions:

1. Whisk melted butter, cream cheese, and eggs in a bowl.

2. Mix the remaining ingredients separately except for blueberries and then add them to the egg mixture from step one and combine it with a batter. Leave it for a few minutes.

3. Place a cast-iron pan or small nonstick pan on medium heat and fry the pancakes. Take 1/3 cup of batter for every pancake.

4. Fry for a few minutes before adding blueberries. Add blueberries and lightly press. Turn over and fry for a few more minutes.

5. Serve with browned butter or whipped cream.

Carbs: 7g, Fat: 44g, Protein: 15g, Calories: 480 kcal

Keto coconut pancakes

Servings: 4

Ingredients:

- 6 eggs

- ¾ cup of coconut milk

- ½ cup coconut flour

- 2 tablespoons melted coconut oil

- 1 pinch salt

- 1 tsp baking powder

- coconut oil or butter for frying

Cooking instructions:

1. Whisk the egg whites separately from the yolks. Use a hand mixer to mix thoroughly with a pinch of salt. Whip until

stiff peaks appear and then put aside.

2.   Use another bowl to whisk a mixture of oil, yolks, and coconut milk.

3.   Add baking powder and coconut flour. Mix carefully to form a batter.

4.   Carefully add the egg whites into the batter and let it rest for five minutes.

5.   Fry for a couple of minutes in coconut oil or butter on both sides on low-medium heat.

6.   Serve with fresh berries and melted butter.

Advice:

Do not pinch on the fat in the frying pan. Coconut oil and butter make it taste better. You can add a spoonful of sour cream on top to make it more delicious.

Carbs: 3g, Fat: 24g, Protein: 12g, Calories: 290 kcal

Low-carb pancakes with berries and whipped cream

Servings: 4

Ingredients:

Toppings

- ½ cup fresh raspberries or fresh strawberries or fresh blueberries

- 4 eggs

- 1 cup heavy whipping cream

- 1 tablespoon ground psyllium husk powder

- 7 oz. cottage cheese

- 2 oz. butter or coconut oil

Cooking instructions:

1. Place eggs, psyllium husk, and cottage cheese into a medium-sized bowl and mix. Let it rest for about 5-10 minutes to form a thick batter.

2. Heat butter or oil in a non-stick pan. Fry the pancakes for 3-4 minutes on a medium to low heat on both sides. Form medium-sized pancakes for easy flipping.

3. Add cream to another bowl. Whip to form soft peaks.

4. Serve the pancakes while hot with whipped cream adding any berries you like.

Advice:

If you need a light and fluffy pancake, then you can separate eggs, but this will take some of your time. Make egg yolks mixture from step one. Whip the egg whites in a separate bowl. Add the egg whites to the batter, gently and carefully folding them in so that they would retain the air which you whipped into them.

Serving suggestions

You can try out serving them with raspberry jam, hazelnut spread, or buttercream.

Carbs: 5g, Fat: 39g, Protein: 13g, Calories: 425 kcal

Keto oatmeal

Servings: 1

Ingredients:

- 1 cup unsweetened almond milk

- 1 tablespoon flax meal

- 1/2 cup hemp hearts

- 1 tablespoon coconut flakes

- 1 tablespoon chia seeds

- 1 tablespoon coconut oil and stevia

- 1 teaspoon cinnamon

Cooking instructions:

1. Add all the ingredients to a sizeable sauce pot and stir to mix.

2. Bring to a simmer until you achieve the desired thickness, stirring occasionally.

3. Serve with frozen berries.

Carbs: 17g, Fat: 44g, Protein: 31g, Calories: 585 kcal

Scrambled eggs in a mug

Are you running out of time? Think about it! A couple of minutes and your breakfast is ready. This is the quickest way of preparing one of the most delicious keto dishes.

Servings:1

Ingredients:

- 2 eggs

- 2 tbsp heavy whipping cream

- 1 tbsp butter

- salt and pepper

Cooking instructions:

1. Grease a mug or cup with soft butter. Whisk eggs with whipping cream. Fill the cup to 2/3 as the eggs will enlarge upon cooking.

2.   Add black pepper (freshly ground) and a pinch of salt to make it especially tasty. Feel free to add your favorite spices.

3.   Put in a microwave and set the power to maximum. Let it cook for 1-2 minutes. Take it out, stir and microwave for the next one minute. Do not overdo them as eggs continue cooking even after they are no longer heating.

4.   Take them out of the microwave and serve after cooling for one minute.

Tip!

Serve the scrambled eggs with finely sliced chives, tuna, and slices of bell pepper to make it a more nutritious meal.

You can skip cream if you don't eat dairy products.

Carbs: 1g, Fat: 31g, Protein: 12g, Calories: 330 kcal

Low-carb mushroom omelet

Servings: 1

Ingredients:

- 3 eggs

- 1 oz. shredded cheese

- 1 oz. butter, for frying

- 3 mushrooms

- 1/5 yellow onion

- salt and pepper

Cooking instructions:

1. Take a mixing bowl and break three eggs into it. Add a pinch of pepper and salt. Use a fork to whisk the eggs until they froth.

2.   Add salt and favorite spices to taste.

3. Chop mushrooms and onions.

4.   Heat a frying pan and melt butter. Pour in the egg mixture.

5.   Let the omelet cook to get a bit firm then sprinkle shredded cheese, mushroom, and onion on top.

6.   Pry the edges of the omelet carefully using a spatula and fold it in half. When the bottom side turns golden brown, take the pan out of the heat.

Tip!

The omelet can be served with a green salad or vinaigrette dressing on the side.

Carbs: 4g, Fat: 43g, Protein: 25g, Calories: 510 kcal

Classic bacon and eggs

Servings: 2

Ingredients:

- 4 eggs

- 2½ oz. bacon slices

- cherry tomatoes (an option)

- fresh parsley (an option)

Cooking instructions:

1. Fry the bacon in a pan at medium heat until it is crispy. Put it on a plate leaving the fat in the pan.

2. Place the same pan over medium heat and crack eggs into the bacon fat.

3. Fry the eggs the way you like. To slightly cook them—

flip the eggs over in a couple of minutes and cook for a minute or leave to fry on one side but use a lid to cover your pan to let the other side get cooked. Cut the tomatoes in half and cook them in the same pan.

4. Add some spices, salt, and pepper to taste.

Tip!

It is recommended to use organic bacon if you can buy it.

Carbs: 1g, Fat: 22g, Protein: 15g, Calories: 270 kcal

Lox omelet

Servings: 1

Ingredients:

- 3 large eggs

- 2 oz. smoked salmon

- 1 tbsp coconut cream or heavy whipping cream

- 1 tbsp butter or ghee

- 1 tbsp fresh dill, minced

- 1 scallion, shaved

- 1 tsp bagel seasoning

Cooking instructions:

1. Preheat a medium skillet at medium heat.

2. Add eggs and cream to a bowl and mix them

thoroughly with a whisk.

3.   Place butter into a pan and melt it, swirl the pan to spread the butter over the entire surface. Add eggs when sizzling stops and let them spread out all over the pan.

4.   Mix up the eggs with a whisk or a spatula. Do not scramble a thin layer of eggs. Just make them fluffy.

5.   Turn off the heat.

6.   Put dill, smoked salmon, and the biggest part of the scallion along with the eggs, then lift one side of the eggs using a spatula and roll it forward the filling to have a tube-like shape.

7.   Put the omelet on a plate and serve with the remaining scallion and bagel seasoning.

Carbs: 2g, Fat: 36g, Protein: 52g, Calories: 540 kcal

Keto Mexican scrambled eggs

Servings: 4

Ingredients:

- 6 eggs

- 1 scallion

- 2 finely chopped, pickled jalapeños

- 1 tomato, finely chopped

- 2 tbsp butter, for frying

- 3 oz. shredded cheese

- salt and pepper

Cooking instructions:

1.   Finely slice tomatoes, scallions, and jalapeños. Mix them and fry in butter for 3 minutes on medium heat.

2.   Whip up eggs in a bowl then pour into the pan. Scramble for two minutes and add seasoning and cheese.

Tip!

Serve with crisp lettuce and avocado to add even more taste to this perfect meal.

Spinach and feta breakfast scramble

Scrambled eggs are the simplest low-carb breakfast that you can easily change according to your tastes. You can add all sorts of spices to achieve your desired taste. To make them taste like a Mediterranean meal, just add some feta and fresh spinach.

Servings: 2

Ingredients:

- 4 large eggs

- 2 tbsp heavy whipping cream

- 2 tbsp butter

- 1 garlic clove, minced

- 4 oz. fresh baby spinach

- ¼ cup feta cheese, crumbled

- 4 oz. bacon (optional)

- Salt and ground black pepper

Cooking instructions:

1. Whisk eggs and cream in a medium bowl to get a well-combined mixture.

2. Preheat a large skillet on medium heat, then add butter and melt it. Stir garlic and spinach. Cook until spinach is wilted then sprinkle with some salt and pepper.

3. Pour the egg mixture into the skillet. Let it cook without disturbing until it begins to set at the edges. Gently lift and turn curds from the edges of the pan towards the center using a rubber spatula. Move the eggs that are uncooked closer to the center. Turn of the heat when eggs are cooked the way you like.

4. Put the eggs to a plate and sprinkle with feta cheese. Serve while hot. You can add some fried bacon if you like.

Carbs: 1g, Fat: 31g, Protein: 12g, Calories: 330 kcal

Scrambled eggs

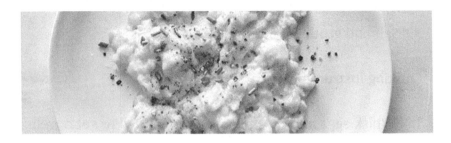

Butter and eggs are perfect for keto breakfast to begin your day. They take just a couple of minutes to cook!

Servings: 1

Ingredients:

- 1 oz butter

- 2 eggs

- salt and pepper

Cooking instructions:

1. Crack eggs into a bowl and whisk them together with a pinch of salt and pepper using a fork.

2. Put a non-stick skillet over medium heat and melt butter. Be very careful because butter should not turn brown.

3.   Pour the egg mixture into the skillet and stir continuously for 1-2 minutes. Cook to your taste, but remember that the eggs will continue cooking even after you turn off the heat.

Tip!

These breakfast pairs well with lots of low-carb favorites. The most common ones are sausage or bacon. However, you can also try cold cuts like avocado, salmon, and cheese.

You can also add more butter and eggs if you are really hungry. Don't be shy!

Carbs: 1g, Fat: 31g, Protein: 12g, Calories: 330 kcal

Boiled eggs with mayonnaise

Servings: 1

Ingredients:

- 2 eggs

- 2 tbsp mayonnaise

- avocado (optional)

Cooking instructions:

1. Place a pot with water over high heat to boil water.

2. Make small holes in the eggs using an egg piercer (optional).

3. Boil eggs for 5-6, 6-8, and 8-10 minutes for soft-boiled eggs, medium-boiled eggs, and hard-boiled eggs.

4. Serve with mayonnaise when cooked.

Tip!

You can serve your eggs with avocado or fried asparagus with homemade mayonnaise. Another simple way of serving is the eggs with butter. Mix them in a small bowl. Add fresh herbs if you wish.

Piercing of eggs prevents them from cracking while boiling.

Carbs: 1g, Fat: 31g, Protein: 12g, Calories: 330 kcal

Meals

Chicken

Keto fried chicken with cabbage

Servings: 2

Ingredients:

- 12 oz. green cabbage

- 3½ oz. butter

- 10 oz. boneless chicken thighs

- salt and pepper

Cooking instructions:

1. Shred the cabbage into fine slices using a food processor or a sharp knife.

2. Heat up a dollop of butter in a large frying pan to place both the chicken and the cabbage in it later.

3. Season the chicken. Use medium heat to fry for 4 minutes on both sides until fully cooked and turns golden brown.

4. Add more butter and cabbage to the pan and fry for the next 5 minutes.

5. Season the cabbage and then serve with the remaining butter.

Tip!

You can cook this keto dish with other low-carb vegetables such as spinach, broccoli, and zucchini. Use any spice you like to add flavor. Chili and paprika powder, some herbs, curry powder, or perhaps onion and/or garlic powder can all fit this dish.

Carbs: 6g, Fat: 66g, Protein: 27g, Calories: 735 kcal

Keto Cream and Chicken Soup

Servings: 6

Ingredients:

- 4 cups chicken broth

- 4 chicken breasts (cooked, boneless, and shredded)

- 1 tsp salt

- 1/2 tsp black pepper

- 1/4 tsp xanthan gum

- 3 tbsp butter

- 2 carrots (chopped)

- 1 onion (chopped)

- 1 cup celery (chopped)

- 2 cups coconut cream or heavy whipping cream

Cooking instructions:

1. Put a saucepan on a medium heat then melt butter in it.

2. Add celery, carrots, onion, pepper, and salt. Saute for five minutes to slightly soften the vegetables.

3. Stir in shredded chicken and then add in the chicken broth and cream.

4. Cook on low-medium heat for 13-15 minutes.

5. Continually stirring add in the xanthan gum. Simmer the soup for 5-6 minutes. You can add more xanthan gum to get a thicker consistency.

6. Serve!

Carbs: 8g, Fat: 35g, Protein: 20g, Calories: 433 kcal

Keto Crispy Fried Chicken

This crunchy fried chicken contains garlic powder, almond flour, and egg to give you that perfect taste and crunch you strive for.

Servings: 2

Ingredients:

- 6 boneless chicken thighs

- 4 oz almond flour or crushed pork rinds

- 2 tsp ground thyme

- 1 tsp garlic powder or 1 tbsp. crushed fresh garlic

- 1 ½ tsp paprika

- ¼ tsp black pepper

- ¼ tsp ground cayenne pepper

- ¼ cup mayonnaise

- 1 egg

- 1 tbsp mustard

- 2 tbsp hot sauce

- 2 tsp salt

Cooking instructions:

1.   Preheat the oven to 425 F. Line a baking rack with either aluminum foil or parchment paper.

2.   Dry the chicken with paper towels and set aside.

3.   Combine all the dry ingredients in a small mixing bowl. Spread a half of dry ingredients mix to a small dish.

4.   Mix eggs, mayonnaise, mustard, and hot sauce in a different bowl.

5.   Dip a chicken thigh, one at a time, into the egg wash, then into the mix of dry ingredients. Flip over a couple of times until the chicken is covered in the breading mixture.

6. Put the breaded chicken thigh to the baking rack. The

same applies to other chicken thighs.

7. Bake the chicken for 35-40 minutes depending on the size of the chicken thighs or until the internal temperature reaches 165 F.

8. Allow to cool slightly and serve.

Tip!

Don't worry if you can't get the pork rinds! You can use almond meal or coconut flour as an alternative.

This recipe can also be used in an air fryer or deep fryer with keto-friendly oils such as tallow, lard, and duck fat.

Carbs: 2g, Fat: 69g, Protein: 123g, Calories: 1115 kcal

Pork

Keto pork chops with blue-cheese sauce

Servings: 4

Ingredients:

- 4 pork chops

- 2 tbsp butter

- 5 oz. blue cheese

- ¾ cup crème fraîche or heavy whipping cream

- 7 oz. fresh green beans

- salt and pepper

Cooking instructions:

1. Place a small pot on medium heat and crumble the

cheese into it. Adjust heat as necessary to melt cheese gently. Be careful not to burn the cheese.

2.   Add either cream or crème fraiche to the melted cheese and increase the temperature slightly. Let it simmer for a couple of minutes.

3.   Add salt and pepper to the chops.

4.   Fry for 2-3 minutes in a skillet on medium-high heat before turning it over. Continue cooking until the internal temperature reaches 145-160F. Place it aside and cover with an aluminum foil for 2-3 minutes.

5.   Add the pan juices to the cheese sauce and stir gently. Warm it up if necessary.

6.   Taste the sauce to check if it needs more salt as blue cheese is often fairly salty.

7.   Trim then rinse the green beans. Fry them in butter on medium heat for 2-3 minutes. Sprinkle with a pinch of salt and pepper.

Tip!

This is an incredibly versatile meal. Feel free to use any kind of meat. Try out the beef, pork, lamb, or even turkey and chicken. Meat and sauce combination will definitely make this dish sing!

Carbs: 4g, Fat: 64g, Protein: 61g, Calories: 850 kcal

Keto pork and green pepper stir-fry

Servings: 2

Ingredients:

- 10 oz. pork shoulder, slices

- 2 scallions

- 2 green bell peppers

- 4 oz. butter

- 1 tsp chili paste

- 2 tbsp almonds

- salt and pepper

Cooking instructions:

1.   Slice scallions and bell pepper. Prepare the pork and cut it into thin strips. Add plenty of butter into a wok or a

frying pan and heat it up. Don't forget to save some butter for serving.

2.   Fry the meat over high heat for 3 minutes until it turns brown then add the chili paste and vegetables. Keep stirring and frying the next couple of minutes. Season with pepper and salt.

3.   Serve while hot with room-temperature butter and almonds.

Tip!

This dish goes well with steak or chicken thigh. So try it out!

Carbs: 5g, Fat: 78g, Protein: 29g, Calories: 840 kcal

Keto Chinese pork stew with cabbage

Servings: 4

Ingredients:

Pork stew

- 1½ lbs of chopped pork shoulder pieces

- 1¾ cups water

- 3 tbsp coconut oil

- 3 tbsp tamari soy sauce

- 2 garlic cloves, minced

- 1 oz. fresh ginger, minced

- 1 star anise

- 1½ lbs Napa cabbage

- salt and ground black pepper

For serving

- 2 scallions, sliced

- 1 tbsp sesame oil

Cooking instructions:

1. Put a heavy-bottomed saucepan over high heat, add coconut oil, and fry the meat for 3-4 minutes to get a nice color. Add salt and pepper.

2. Add other ingredients except for cabbage. Set a medium-low heat, cover with a lid and simmer for 40-45 minutes or until the meat becomes soft. Take away the star anise before you serve. Season with salt and pepper.

3. Shred the cabbage and fry in coconut oil until it turns golden brown. Add pepper and salt to taste.

4. Serve the stew with sliced scallions, sesame oil, and cabbage.

Tip!

Feel free to serve the stew with a different side dish. You can use cauliflower rice, zoodles or butter-fried green cabbage if you want.

You can use chicken, beef or lamb if you don't eat pork.

Carbs: 4g, Fat: 44g, Protein: 33g, Calories: 560 kcal

Smoked ham stuffed zucchini boats

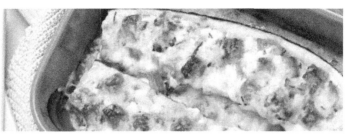

Servings: 4

Ingredients:

- 2 zucchini

- 1 tbsp olive oil

- 1 tsp salt

- 15 oz. smoked deli ham

- 2 tbsp mayonnaise

- 4 oz. cottage cheese

- 2 tbsp finely chopped red onions

- ½ tbsp dried rosemary

- 1½ cups shredded cheese

- salt and pepper

For serving

- 7 oz. lettuce

- 4 tbsp olive oil

- ½ tbsp white wine vinegar

- salt and pepper

Cooking instructions:

1. Preheat oven to 400°F.

2. Cut all the zucchini in halves along the length and take out the seeds. Sprinkle salt on top and let it rest for 10 minutes.

3. Use a paper towel to remove the liquid drops. Put the halves in a baking dish greased with olive oil.

4. Chop ham into big pieces and mix together with cottage cheese, red onions, mayonnaise, and spices. Add 1/3 of the grated cheese. Sprinkle some pepper and salt to taste.

5. Spread the mixture into the zucchini halves and sprinkle the cheese on top. Bake for about 20-30 minutes or until you get a desired golden-brown color.

6.   Chop the lettuce coarsely. Make a mix of oil, vinegar, salt, and pepper. Use this mix to season the lettuce. Serve the zucchini beside a simple salad.

Carbs: 7g, Fat: 39g, Protein: 33g, Calories: 515 kcal

Beef

Keto ground beef and broccoli

One-skillet magic: real food, simple ingredients, easy to prepare, and a tasty dinner. It's ketogenic fast food that can be easily made in your kitchen. Give it a try!

Servings: 2

Ingredients:

- 10 oz. ground beef

- 3 oz. butter

- 9 oz. broccoli

- salt and pepper

- ½ cup crème fraîche or mayonnaise (optional)

Cooking instructions:

1.   Rinse broccoli. Trim and cut it into small florets. Don't throw away the stem, peel it and cut into pieces.

2.   Melt a dollop of butter in a frying pan which is big enough for both the ground beef and broccoli.

3.   Use high heat to fry the ground beef until it turns golden brown then add salt and pepper to taste.

4.   Add more butter, lower the heat, and add broccoli. Fry while stirring for another 3-5 minutes.

5.   Season the broccoli. Top with butter and serve while hot. You can also serve with a dollop of mayonnaise or crème fraiche.

Tip!

You can cook this keto dish with many other low-carb veggies such as spinach, green beans, asparagus, and zucchini. Try flavoring it with chili and paprika powder, herbs, or onion powder.

Carbs: 5g, Fat: 54g, Protein: 33g, Calories: 648 kcal

Keto cheeseburger

Servings: 4

Ingredients:

Salsa

- 2 tomatoes

- 2 scallions

- 1 avocado

- salt

- 1 tbsp olive oil

- fresh cilantro, to taste

Burgers

- 1½ lbs ground beef

- 7 oz. shredded cheese

- 2 oz. butter, for frying

- 2 tsp garlic powder

- 2 tsp paprika powder

- 2 tsp onion powder

- 2 tbsp fresh and finely chopped oregano

Toppings

- 5 oz. lettuce

- 5 oz. cooked, crumbled bacon

- ½ cup sliced dill pickles

- ¼ cup pickled jalapeños

- ¾ cup mayonnaise

- 4 tbsp Dijon mustard

Cooking instructions:

1.   Chop all the salsa ingredients and place them in a small bowl and stir together. Set aside.

2.   Mix half of the cheese and seasoning with the ground

beef, do it with your hands until everything is fully blended.

3.   Make four burgers and fry over high heat in a pan using butter. You can also grill them if you like. Add the rest of the cheese on top when almost ready.

4.   Serve on lettuce with bacon, pickled jalapeños, mayo, dill pickle, and mustard. Don't forget to use your homemade salsa!

Carbs: 8g, Fat: 104g, Protein: 53g, Calories: 1195 kcal

Stuffed peppers with cheese and ground beef

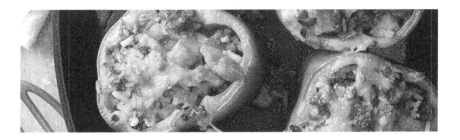

Servings: 4

Ingredients:

- 1 oz. butter (for baking dish greasing)

- 4 green bell peppers

- 4 tbsp olive oil

- 2 garlic cloves

- 1 yellow onion

- 1½ lbs ground beef

- 2 tsp ground cumin

- 2 tsp chili powder

- 7 oz. crushed tomatoes

- ½ lb shredded cheese

- 4 oz. leafy greens

- salt and pepper

- 1 cup sour cream or mayonnaise

Cooking instructions:

1. Preheat the oven to 400°F (200°C).

2. Cut the peppers lengthwise into two halves and remove seeds. Grease a baking dish and place peppers in it.

3. Sprinkle olive oil on the peppers and start baking them while you prepare the filling. If you prefer a crunchy pepper, skip this step and start baking when filled.

4. Finely chop the garlic and onion.

5. Place a frying pan over medium heat, drizzle some olive oil and the chopped garlic and onions. Fry until soft and add the ground beef. Stir when stirring for about 5 minutes

6. Add cumin, chili, crushed tomatoes, pepper, and salt. Simmer for 10 minutes.

7. Turn off the heat. Stir in half of the cheese.

8.   Add the beef mix to the peppers. Sprinkle cheese on top and place in the oven.

9.   Bake for 25 minutes or until the cheese has melted.

10.   Serve with some leafy greens and a dollop of sour cream.

Carbs: 13g, Fat: 70g, Protein: 51g, Calories: 897 kcal

Low-carb Goulash soup

This spicy, complex, and rich textured Hungarian dish will totally make the chilly evening warmer.

Servings: 6

Ingredients:

- 1 yellow onion

- 1 red bell pepper

- 2 garlic cloves

- 8 oz. rutabaga or celery root

- 15 oz. ground beef or lamb

- ¼ tsp cayenne pepper

- 1 tbsp paprika powder

- ½ tbsp caraway seeds

- 1 tbsp dried oregano

- 4¼ oz. olive oil or butter

- 1 tsp salt

- 15 oz. crushed tomatoes

- ¼ tsp ground black pepper

- 1½ tsp red wine vinegar

- 2½ - 3 cups of water

For serving

- 1 cup mayonnaise or sour cream

- fresh parsley (for garnish)

Cooking instructions:

1. Peel and chop the vegetables into small pieces.

2. Sauté the garlic and onion, in a heavy pan with butter or oil, over medium heat until softened.

3. Add ground beef or lamb and sauté. Stir occasionally, until it is golden brown and cooked.

4.   Add paprika, cayenne, oregano, bell pepper, celery root, caraway, salt, and pepper. Stir for one minute then pour 2 cups of water and tomatoes.

5.   Bring the soup to a boil and let it simmer for 10 minutes.

6.   Add the vinegar and the remaining water before serving.

7.   Serve with mayonnaise or a dollop of sour cream and finely chopped parsley.

Tip!

Lamb is the best choice for this soup. However, if you don't have any – try ground beef, pork, or even turkey or chicken for a milder flavor.

Carbs: 11g, Fat: 42g, Protein: 16g, Calories: 490 kcal

Salmon

Keto fried salmon with asparagus

Super tasty one-skillet dish with just three main ingredients! It's fast to cook, ketogenic, and delicious dinner.

Servings: 2

Ingredients:

- 8 oz. green asparagus

- 9 oz. salmon

- 3 oz. butter

- pepper and salt

Cooking instructions:

1. Finely rinse and trim the asparagus.

2. Melt a dollop of butter in a frying pan large enough to fit both the asparagus and the fish.

3. Use medium heat to fry the asparagus for about 3-4 minutes. Push asparagus away to one half of the pan and season with pepper and salt.

4. Add more butter and fry salmon for 2-3 minutes on each side. Stir the asparagus while cooking the salmon. Lower the heat.

5. Season the salmon before serving. Add some butter on top!

Tip!

You can cook this keto dish with other vegetables like zucchini, cauliflower, spinach, or broccoli. Use your favorite spices such as paprika, onion powder, chili powder, freshly chopped garlic, some herbs.

Carbs: 2g, Fat: 52g, Protein: 28g, Calories: 590 kcal

Keto salmon-filled avocados

Avocado plus smoked salmon equals to no cooking at all. This yummy dish is a nice and fast breakfast, light lunch, or dinner. So easy, delicious, and keto!

Servings: 2

Ingredients:

- 2 avocados

- 6 oz. smoked salmon

- ¾ cup crème fraîche or mayonnaise or sour cream

- salt and pepper

- 2 tbsp lemon juice (as an option)

Cooking instructions:

1. Cut the avocados in half and take out the pits.

2.   Fill the hollow part of the avocado with a dollop of mayonnaise or crème fraiche. Place smoked salmon on top.

3.   Season with pepper and salt to taste. As an option, squeeze lemon juice to add more flavor (and the avocado won't turn brown if you do this).

Tip!

You can serve this colorful keto dish with any other fatty fish - boiled, smoked, or fried. Feel free to use fresh herbs like dill or basil to make this dish sing!

Carbs: 6g, Fat: 71g, Protein: 58g, Calories: 910 kcal

Keto fried salmon with broccoli and cheese

Servings: 4

Ingredients:

- 1 lb broccoli

- 3 oz. butter

- salt and pepper

- 5 oz. cheddar cheese (grated)

- 1½ lbs salmon

- 1 lime (optional)

Cooking instructions:

1. Preheat the oven to 200°C (400°F), use broiler settings if possible.

2. Cut broccoli into small florets and simmer in slightly

salted water for 2-3 min. Make sure the broccoli keeps its delicate color and chewy texture.

3. Drain the boiling water and set the broccoli aside, uncovered, for about 1-2 minutes.

4. Lay the drained broccoli into a greased baking dish. Add some pepper and butter to taste.

5. Sprinkle cheddar cheese on top of the broccoli. Bake it in the oven for about 15-20 minutes, until the cheese turns into a golden color.

6. Meanwhile, season the salmon with pepper and salt. Fry it in a heavy pan over medium-high heat in plenty of butter. 2-3 minutes for each side. You can serve it with raw lime or fry lime in the same pan.

Tip!

You can use green beans, Brussels sprouts, or asparagus as an alternative to broccoli and have no changes in the number of carbs.

Other fatty fishes, including trout and mackerel, can be used as a substitute to salmon.

Cheddar is easily replaceable too. Just try a mix of parmesan and mozzarella!

Carbs: 6g, Fat: 52g, Protein: 46g, Calories: 685 kcal

Other meals

Keto fried halloumi cheese with mushrooms

All you need to cook a tasty and filling keto meal is some seasoning, four ingredients, and only 15 minutes. Enjoy!

Servings: 2

Ingredients:

- 10 oz. mushrooms

- 10 oz. halloumi cheese

- 3 oz. butter

- 10 green olives

- salt and pepper

- ½ cup mayonnaise (optional)

Cooking instructions:

1. Rinse, trim and slice mushrooms.

2. Heat up a frying pan that will fit both mushrooms and halloumi cheese and melt a hearty dollop of butter.

3. Use medium heat to fry the mushrooms until they are golden brown or for 3-5 minutes. Season with pepper and salt.

4. Fry halloumi for 2-3 minutes each side, add some butter if needed. Stir the mushrooms while the cheese is cooking. Lower the heat. Serve with olives.

Tip!

Feel free to use the other low-carb vegetables like zucchini, broccoli, asparagus, and spinach. Spices will also give great flavor to this dish – paprika and chili powder, some onion powder and herbal seasoning, or maybe basil and garlic.

Carbs: 7g, Fat: 74g, Protein: 36g, Calories: 830 kcal

Keto pizza

As I'm a pizza fan, here is a simple way of making a low-carb pizza. Fast and simple. Excellent flavor mix of cheese, tomato sauce, and pepperoni make it delicious. I hope you'll love it!

Servings: 2

Ingredients:

Crust

- 4 eggs

- 6 oz. cheese (shredded provolone or mozzarella)

Topping

- 3 tbsp unsweetened tomato sauce

- 1 tsp dried oregano

- 1½ oz. pepperoni

- 5 oz. shredded cheese

- olives (as an option)

For serving

- 4 tbsp olive oil

- 2 oz. leafy greens

- ground black pepper and sea salt

Cooking instructions:

1.   Preheat the oven to 200°C (400°F).

2.   Cooking starts with making the crust. Crack the eggs into a bowl and stir them. Add shredded cheese and mix together with the eggs.

3.   Line a baking sheet with a parchment paper and spread egg and cheese batter on it using a spatula. You can choose to make two round or one large rectangular crust. Bake for about 15 minutes or until the crust turns golden. Remove from heat and let it cool for a couple of minutes.

4.   Increase the heat to 225°C (450°F).

5.   Spread the tomato sauce on the crust. Top with oregano and cheese, then place the olives and pepperoni on top.

6.   Bake in the oven for about 5-10 minutes or until turns golden-brown.

7.   Serve with a fresh salad.

Carbs: 5g, Fat: 90g, Protein: 53g, Calories: 1045 kcal

Low-carb frittata with fresh spinach

Servings: 4

Ingredients:

- 5 oz. diced bacon or chorizo

- 8 oz. fresh spinach

- 2 tbsp butter

- 1 cup heavy whipping cream

- 8 eggs

- 5 oz. shredded cheese

- salt and pepper

Cooking instructions:

1.   Preheat the oven to 175°C (350°F) and grease a 9 x 9 baking dish or the ramekins.

2.   Use medium heat to melt the butter and fry the bacon until crispy. Add the spinach and continue stirring until wilted. Set the pan aside.

3.   Whisk cream and the eggs together. Pour the mixture into a baking dish or ramekins.

4.   Add spinach, cheese, and bacon on top. Place the baking dish in the middle of the oven. Bake until golden-brown color or for 25-30 minutes.

Tip!

Serve with red cabbage or shredded green on the side, use homemade dressing!

Carbs: 4g, Fat: 59g, Protein: 27g, Calories: 660 kcal

Sausage stroganoff with cauliflower and parsley rice

Servings: 4

Ingredients:

- 1 yellow onion

- 1 red bell pepper

- 2 oz. butter

- 1 lb chorizo or another high-quality sausage

- 1 oz. sun-dried tomatoes in olive oil

- 2 tbsp tomato paste

- 1 tbsp Dijon mustard

- 2 tbsp dried thyme

- 1¼ cups sour cream or heavy whipping cream

- salt and pepper

Fried cauliflower and parsley rice

- 1½ lbs cauliflower

- ¼ cup chopped fresh parsley

- 4 oz. butter

Cooking instructions:

1.   Melt butter in a pan and fry sausage until fully cooked. Set aside to cool.

2.   Cut the onion and bell pepper in thin slices.

3.   Fry the onion and pepper over medium heat in the pan that was used for the sausage.

4.   Cut the sausage to make bite-sized pieces and place them in the pan with the onion and pepper. Don't forget to stir while frying for another minute.

5.   Add Dijon mustard, dry thyme, and heavy whipping cream. Lower the heat to a medium-low when boiling begins and simmer for 10-15 minutes. Add salt and pepper to taste.

6.   Serve with cauliflower and parsley rice.

Cauliflower and parsley rice

1.   Use the coarse side of a grater to shred the cauliflower. You can shred it using a food processor, but don't make it too finely shredded.

2.   Melt the butter in a large frying pan. Stir and fry the cauliflower on high heat for 3-4 minutes. Add chopped parsley and season with salt and pepper before serving.

Tip!

You can use meat instead of sausages, so try beef, turkey, or chicken. Add some seasoning to the meat. For that purpose, use paprika, garlic, and dry herbs.

Carbs: 16g, Fat: 107g, Protein: 35g, Calories: 1170 kcal

Keto cheese roll-ups

Servings: 4

Ingredients:

- 8 oz. cheddar cheese or Edam cheese or provolone cheese, in slices

- 2 oz. butter

- 1 pinch paprika powder

Cooking instructions:

1. Transfer the sliced pieces of cheese onto a large cutting board.

2. Slice butter into thin pieces using a cheese slicer or a knife.

3. Cover each cheese slice with butter and then roll them up. Serve as a snack.

Tip!

Cheese rolls are already very tasty in themselves, but you can also include some additives into this recipe. You can try any of the following: salt flakes, paprika powder, fresh herbs, or finely chopped parsley.

Carbs: 2g, Fat: 42g, Protein: 16g, Calories: 335 kcal

Low-carb mushroom soup

Servings: 4

Ingredients:

Soup:

- 1 yellow onion

- 3 oz. Parma ham

- 1 lb mushrooms

- 4 oz. butter

- 1 tsp dried thyme

- 1 tsp ground or sea salt kosher

- ¼ tsp ground black pepper

- 1/3 cup dry white wine

- 7 oz. cream cheese

- 2 cups of water

- 1 cup heavy whipping cream

- 4 egg yolks

Parsley oil:

- ½ cup olive oil

- 1 oz. fresh parsley

- pepper and salt

Cooking instructions:

1. Preheat the oven to 150°C (300°F). Use the oven's convection setting if possible.

2. Line a baking sheet with a parchment paper and put in sliced Parma ham. Place on the top rack of the oven to bake. Check the ham out every 5 minutes and flip it for a couple of times. Wait till the ham crisps up. It will take about 30 minutes.

3. Saute mushrooms and onions in butter until they turn golden. Better use a thick bottom pot. Season with salt, thyme, and pepper to taste.

4.   Add wine, water, cheese and stir the soup. Bring to a boil for some minutes, then set the heat to medium and let simmer for another 15 minutes.

5.   Whisk the heavy cream thoroughly until there are soft peaks formed, add yolks and mix it well.

6.   Add egg cream into the soup. No further boiling is required.

7.   Add parsley, oil, pepper, and salt in a tall beaker. Use your immersion blender until your mixture is merged together or for about 30 seconds.

8.   Serve your soup with Parma-ham crisp and parsley oil.

Tip!

Add flavor by including either water or white wine. You can also try hard liquor such as vermouth, cognac, or dry port wine. You can change the quantities accordingly to taste. You can also skip wine and liquor and just use a mix of green oil and lemon juice.

Carbs: 11g, Fat: 95g, Protein: 15g, Calories: 960 kcal

Salads

Greek salad

Servings: 2

Ingredients:

- 3 ripe tomatoes

- ½ red onion

- ½ green bell pepper

- ½ cucumber

- 7 oz. feta cheese

- 10 black Greek olives

- ½ tbsp red wine vinegar

- 4 tbsp olive oil

- 2 tsp dried oregano

- pepper and salt

Cooking instructions:

1.   Cut the cucumber and tomatoes into medium pieces. Slice the bell pepper and the onion into thin pieces. Place the salad on the serving plates.

2.   Add olives and feta cheese, then drizzle vinegar and olive oil over the salad.

3.   Sprinkle with crumbled oregano on top and season with pepper and salt to taste. Serve.

Tip!

Need a different look? You can try cherry tomatoes. Add more colors! Use yellow tomatoes with red or orange bell peppers. Or just crumble the feta to achieve a different presentation with a similar taste.

Carbs: 15g, Fat: 51g, Protein: 17g, Calories: 585 kcal

Spicy shrimp salad

Servings: 4

Ingredients:

- ½ lime, juice

- 2 avocados

- 2 oz. baby spinach

- 5 oz. cucumber

- 3 tbsp olive oil, for frying

- 2 tsp chili powder or sambal oelek

- 1 garlic pressed clove

- 10 oz. peeled shrimp

- fresh cilantro

- 2 tbsp salted peanuts or hazelnuts (optional)

Ginger dressing

- 1 tbsp minced fresh ginger

- ¼ cup light olive oil or avocado oil

- ½ lime, juice

- ½ pressed garlic clove

- ½ tbsp soy sauce

- pepper and salt

Cooking instructions:

1. Split the avocado into halves to remove the pit. Peel the avocado and cut it into slices. Squeeze lime over the avocado. Peel a cucumber and slice it.

2. Take a plate and combine avocado, spinach, and cucumber. Season the salad with salt.

3. Use a pan to fry chili and garlic in oil. Fry shrimps for a couple of minutes on each side if raw. If you use pre-cooked shrimps, just heat them up quickly. Season with pepper and salt to taste.

4.   Put shrimps on the vegetables. Sprinkle with cilantro and nuts.

5.   Take immersion blender to mix the dressing ingredients and drizzle over salad.

Carbs: 9g, Fat: 79g, Protein: 26g, Calories: 870kcal

Keto Asian beef salad

Servings: 2

Ingredients:

Sesame mayonnaise

- ¾ cup mayonnaise

- 1 tsp sesame oil

- ½ tbsp lime juice

- salt and pepper

Beef

- 1 tablespoon olive oil

- 1 tablespoon fish sauce

- 1 tablespoon grated fresh ginger

- 1 teaspoon chili flakes

- 2/3 lb ribeye steaks

Salad

- 2 oz. cucumber

- 3 oz. cherry tomatoes

- 3 oz. lettuce

- ½ red onion

- fresh cilantro

- 2 scallions

- 1 tsp sesame seeds

Cooking instructions:

1. Mix egg yolk and mustard in a bowl to prepare sesame mayonnaise.

2. Add avocado oil in a slow stream without stopping whisking. It can be done manually or with the help of a hand mixer or blender. Pour oil, juice of lime and spice up closer to the end as soon as mayonnaise is emulsified.

3. Make a mixture with all ingredients needed for the

marinade and transfer it to a special plastic bag. Toss beef, marinade for about 15 minutes, room temperature.

4.   All vegetables but for green onions should be cut into tiny pieces. Split them up on two separate plates.

5.   Heat your pan on medium heat. Dry your pan, sesame seeds on it, toast for a few minutes or wait till they are of light brown color and fragrant. Put aside.

6.   Next, pat meat so it would become dry from both sides using special paper towels. Fry for one to two minutes on each separate side on high heat turned on, or until it is ready on medium heat. (In this dish, the beef tastes the best when prepared on medium heat. Still, you can cook it more thoroughly.)

7.   1 minute to fry green onion using the same pan.

8.   Cut meat in thin slices. Top vegetables with beef and green onions. You can serve with fried sesame and sesame mayonnaise.

Carbs: 7g, Fat: 96g, Protein: 33g, Calories: 1025kcal

Roasted tomato salad

Servings: 4

Ingredients:

- 3 tablespoons of olive oil

- 1 lb cherry tomatoes

- 1 tablespoon of sea salt

- 1/2 tablespoon of ground black pepper

- 1/2 cup of well-chopped scallions

- 1 tablespoon of red wine vinegar

Cooking instructions:

1. Cover tomatoes with oil and sprinkle them with spices.

2. Cook on the grill with the help of a special vegetable accessory, or in the oven, as a possible option, until the

tomatoes are browned a bit.

3.   If you are using the oven, bake at 450F (225C) for about 15 minutes. Then stir, turn the oven off. However, you should leave the tomatoes to bake for a little longer, that is, around ten more minutes.

4.   Plate and sprinkle chopped scallions on top. Drizzle with vinegar and the rest of the olive oil. Let rest, so the flavors mingle; serve the salad lukewarm or cold.

Tip!

Chop tomatoes in large pieces if you would like to go for a more salsa-like salad. Or you can toss some crumbled feta for additional scents. It's the best decision for virtually any dishes grilled. Summer, we are coming!

Carbs: 4g, Fat: 10g, Protein: 1g, Calories: 114kcal

Tuna salad with poached eggs

Servings: 2

Ingredients:

Tuna Salad

- 4 oz. tuna in olive oil, drained

- 1/3 cup of chopped celery stalks

- 1/2 red onion

- 1/2 cup of mayonnaise

- 1 tablespoon of Dijon mustard

- 1/2 lemon, juice and zest

- salt and pepper

- 2 tablespoons of small capers

- 2 oz. leafy greens or lettuce

- 2 oz. cherry tomatoes

- 2 tablespoons of olive oil

Poached eggs

- 4 eggs

- 1 tablespoon salt

- 2 tablespoons of white wine or white vinegar 5%

Cooking instructions:

1. Mix the peeled tuna with other components of this salad, with the exception of lettuce and tomatoes. You may do this step in advance, then store this mixture in the refrigerator for a few days, and this really helps flavors open up.

2. Slightly boil water. Add salt and vinegar. Stir the water in a circle, thus creating a swirl. Break eggs by one.

3. Leave it to simmer for 2 minutes, then take out of the water with the help of a slotted spoon.

4. It can be served along with fresh herbs and a few tomatoes. Before serving, sprinkle this dish with olive oil.

Tip!

In case you think poaching eggs sound too complicated, then change them with boiled eggs. Boil eggs for 7 minutes, after that, cool them in cold water before starting to peel them.

Carbs: 6g, Fat: 69g, Protein: 29g, Calories: 766kcal

Desserts

Low-carb chocolate and peanut squares

Servings: 12

Ingredients:

- 31⁄2 oz. dark chocolate, minimum 70% cocoa solids

- 4 tablespoons of butter or coconut oil

- 1 pinch salt

- 1⁄4 cup peanut butter

- 1⁄2 tablespoons of vanilla extract

- 1 tablespoon licorice powder, ground cinnamon, or ground cardamom (green)

- 1⁄4 cup cut salted peanuts as a decoration

Cooking instructions:

1. Melt chocolate and butter or coconut oil in a microwave or in a steamer. In case there is no double boiler, you can place a glass bowl on a pan with boiling water. Check that the water would not enter this bowl. The steam heat is to melt chocolate. Put melted chocolate away and let it cool down for a few minutes before moving onto the next part.

2. Add all other ingredients left but for nuts, mix till completely dissolved.

3. Pour the dough onto a small buttered baking dish with parchment paper (of approximately 4 x 6 inches).

4.Put well-cut peanuts or other original fillings on top. Transfer to the fridge to cool.

5.Once the dough is stiffened, make tiny squares out of it with a sharp knife. Remember to make these and all other sweets in small sizes that are no more than 1 x 1 inch square. The dough is stored in the fridge or a freezer.

Tip

Both almond or nut oil can also be used as an option.

Moreover, you can always try different fillings: toasted (and large cut) almonds or hazelnuts, fried sesame seeds with unsweetened coconut shavings, or even tahini. Delicious!

Carbs: 4g, Fat: 12g, Protein: 3g, Calories: 138kcal

Low-carb nougat sweets

Servings: 40

Ingredients:

• 7½ oz. dark chocolate with a minimum of 80% cocoa solids

• ½ cup coconut oil, divided

• 14 oz. coconut milk, only the solid part

•8 tablespoon peanut butter or any other nut butter that is of your liking

• 1 tablespoon cocoa powder

• 1 teaspoon vanilla extract

Cooking instructions:

1. In a water bath or microwave, melt half the chocolate on

low heat. Then pour coconut oil of one-quarter quantity, stir thoroughly.

2. Transfer onto a greased and parchment-lined mold (about 5 x 8 inches if you're preparing 40 sweets), let it cool down in a fridge or a freezer.

3.Warm up the solid part of coconut milk carefully using another pan. Brew for a couple of minutes.

4. Stirring, put half of the coconut oil into the pan, nut butter, cocoa powder, vanilla. Blend to make a smooth dough. In case it separates, use a hand mixer and pulse several times, thus making it smooth.

5.Take off the heat, pour with chocolate. Transfer the pan again to the refrigerator or freezer so that it cools down and continues melting the rest of the chocolate like in the first step.

6. Mix coconut oil that is left with the chocolate stir. Make a layer over cooled nougat. Return it to the refrigerator and leave it for no less than 1 hour or even longer.

7. Cut into ten small pieces. Use a refrigerator or freezer to store in an airtight container. Best to serve nougat when it is

a little chilled.

Tip!

You can form a water bath by placing a resistant to heat bowl over a pan with boiling water. Do not allow water to get to the pot's bottom. Put the crushed chocolate into a bowl and stir till it melts. Pay attention so that water would not get into your chocolate. Otherwise, it will curdle. You can replace coconut oil with butter or ghee.

Carbs: 3g, Fat: 8g, Protein: 1g, Calories: 86kcal

Low-carb coconut and chocolate pudding

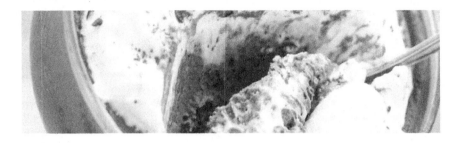

Servings: 6

Ingredients:

- 14 oz. coconut milk

- 2 egg yolks

- 3 oz. dark chocolate with cocoa powder content of at least 70%

- 1 tablespoon of vanilla extract

Cooking instructions:

1. Put coconut milk, egg yolks into a pan, stir to blend them. Turn on medium heat, let the mixture simmer for 10 minutes, stirring.

2. Break the chocolate into small pieces and place these pieces into a bowl.

3. Add vanilla, top with coconut milk. Let it rest for some time so that the chocolate would melt.

4. Beat the dough, pour into glasses

5. Place in the fridge for two hours minimum before you serve the dish

Carbs: 7g, Fat: 22g, Protein: 3g, Calories: 235kcal

Crunchy keto berry mousse

Servings: 8

Ingredients:

- 2 cups of thick whipped cream

- 3 oz. fresh raspberries, strawberries or blueberries

- 2 oz. chopped pecans

- 1/2 lemon zest

- 1/4 tablespoon vanilla extract

Cooking instructions:

1. Pour cream into a special bowl and beat using a hand mixer till soft peaks are appearing. In the end, lemon zest and vanilla should be added.

2. Put berries and nuts into whipped cream then mix

carefully.

3. Use plastic wrap as a cover and transfer to the refrigerator for a period of around 3 hours to get a solid mousse. However, you can also eat the dessert when it is ready unless you are okay with a less firm consistency of it.

Tip!

We like mixing raspberries and blueberries. And what do you like to mix? You can try mixing strawberries, cherries, blackberries, or red and black currants.

Carbs: 3g, Fat: 26g, Protein: 2g, Calories: 256kcal

Low-carb cinnamon apples with vanilla sauce

Servings: 6

Ingredients:

Vanilla sauce

- 21⁄2 cups of thick whipping cream

- 1⁄2 tablespoon of vanilla extract

- 1 star anise (optional)

- 2 tablespoons of butter

- 1 egg yolk

Cinnamon apples

- 3 tablespoons of butter

- 3 apples, if possible of a firm and tart type like Granny

Smith

- 1 tablespoon ground cinnamon

Cooking instructions:

1. Place butter, vanilla, and, if possible, star anise into the saucepan along with a quarter of thick whipped cream. Boil the mix lightly on medium heat. Reduce the heat, let it simmer for around 5 minutes till the sauce is creamy. Stir often.2. Take off the heat, remove the star anise. Whipping, add the egg yolk. Keep the mixture in the fridge until it is cooled down completely. There is a possibility of cooking flavored cream one day in advance and store it in the fridge.

3. Whip thick whipped cream that is left in a bowl till soft peaks form. Pour this into the chilled sauce.

4. Return the mixture back to the fridge for an extra 30 minutes. It is possible to pour the cream sauce into the serving cups in order for it to thicken faster.

5. Rinse apples, peel them if you wish. However, it's peel gives this dish color, texture, flavor.

6. Peel the apple from its core and cut it into thin slices.

Heat the butter in a pan, fry apple slices until they are golden. When finishing, add cinnamon.

7. Serve apples when they are warm along with a vanilla sauce

Tip!

This sauce goes well with various desserts where vanilla custard is usually served. For instance, you can warm up some blackberries or raspberries to serve them later with vanilla sauce. Freeze them to get superb ice cream!

Carbs: 12g, Fat: 47g, Protein: 4g, Calories: 476kcal

Drinks

Low-carb blueberry smoothie

This breakfast is great when on the run because it's both simple and light with the low carbs content. Fresh, fragrant blueberries are perfectly combined with coconut milk, vanilla, lemon juice. You can cook lots of them for your whole family! Just awesome!

Servings: 2

Ingredients:

- 14 oz. of coconut milk

- 1/2 cup of frozen or fresh blueberries

- 1 tablespoon of lemon juice

- 1/2 tablespoon vanilla extract

Cooking instructions:

1. Blend all the components in a blender till smooth. Canned coconut milk makes the cocktail more creamy and delicious.

2. Try it out, pour more lemon juice if you think there is a need to do so.

Tip

Add one tablespoon of coconut oil or any other health-beneficial oil - this will make your smoothie richer. You can replace coconut milk with 1 1/4 cups of Greek yogurt in case you like milkshakes more. Add more water to make the consistency more liquid.

Carbs: 10g, Fat: 43g, Protein: 4g, Calories: 418kcal

Low-carb strawberry smoothie

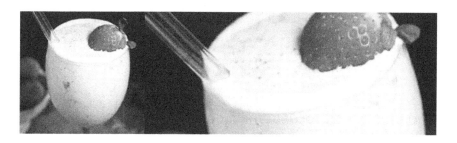

There are times when we just desire smoothies. So this recipe meets all the yummy meal demands. Fresh strawberries, coconut milk, notes of vanilla and lime-can there be anything better? Make sure to prepare enough of them! It's relatively easy to grab and go on a hectic morning!

Servings: 2

Ingredients:

- 14 oz. of coconut milk

- 5 oz. fresh strawberries

- 1 tablespoon of lime juice

- 1/2 teaspoon of vanilla extract

Cooking instructions:

1. Blend all the components until the consistency is

smooth. Canned coconut milk (do not forget to drain the liquid) makes the smoothie more creamy and delicious.

2. Pour lime juice to taste.

Tip

Add one tablespoon of coconut oil or any other health-beneficial oil - this will make your smoothie richer. You can replace coconut milk with 1 1/4 cups of Greek yogurt in case you like milkshakes more. If you do, add more water to make the consistency more liquid. Enjoy!

Carbs: 10g, Fat: 42g, Protein: 5g, Calories: 419kcal

Low-carb ginger smoothie

Servings: 2

Ingredients:

- 1/3 cup of coconut milk or coconut cream

- 2/3 cup of water

- 2 tablespoons lime juice

- 1 oz. frozen spinach

- 2 tablespoons of fresh ginger, grated

Cooking instructions:

1. Mix all ingredients. Start adding lime with one tablespoon, continue to taste.

2. Sprinkle with grated ginger, serve. Delicious!

Tip!

Prepare your cocktails in advance to make your morning hurry easier. They can be stored in the refrigerator for up to 2 days. Use a sealed lid, and don't forget to shake your smoothie well enough before you drink it!

Carbs: 3g, Fat: 8g, Protein: 1g, Calories: 82kcal

Keto coffee

What about butter and oil in a cup of coffee? Why not! Just a couple of sips of this scalding hot keto coffee, and you'll be ready to move mountains. Let's get ready!

Servings: 1

Ingredients:

- 1 cup of hot freshly brewed coffee

- 2 tablespoons of unsalted butter

- 1 tablespoon coconut oil

- cinnamon

- cocoa powder

Cooking instructions:

1. Mix all the ingredients in a blender until you get a

uniform foam.

2. Add a little of unsweetened cocoa powder and cinnamon.

3. Serve coffee as soon as it's ready.

Fat, along with caffeine, will fill up your energy levels to start your day. In case caffeine doesn't fit you, try making it without the caffeine. This will not affect you in the same way, but you will still get a superb taste and filling drink.

The clear advantages of this drink are long-lasting satiation, and full energy level, and perhaps a sense of clarity of mind (thanks to ketones and caffeine).

Carbs: 0g, Fat: 38g, Protein: 1g, Calories: 335kcal

Coffee with cream

So yummy! Hot coffee with thick cream will warm you up to your toes! Drink it in the mornings as a boost of energy, or as a creamy keto dessert.

Servings: 1

Ingredients:

- 3/4 cup coffee, brewed how you like it

- 4 tablespoons heavy whipping cream

Cooking instructions:

1. Prepare your favorite coffee. Pour cream into a small pan and heat gently, stirring till it becomes frothy.

2. Pour warm cream into a large cup, add coffee while continuing stirring. Serve immediately without anything more, or with nuts or a slice of cheese.

Tip!

Add dark chocolate to your coffee cup that contains at least 70% cocoa solids. If you do so, then by the time you drink your coffee, you will have a sweet melted thing. You can also try it with cinnamon that will make it a great and juicy treat after a meal!

Carbs: 2g, Fat: 21g, Protein: 2g, Calories: 201kcal

Chapter 6:

21 day meal plan

Week one

	Breakfast	**Lunch**	**Dinner**
Monday	Scrambled eggs in a mug *Page: 88*	Keto pork chops with blue-cheese sauce *Page: 111*	Keto ground beef and broccoli *Page: 122*
Tuesday	Low-carb blueberry smoothie *Page: 181*	*Leftovers:* Keto ground beef and broccoli *Page: 122*	Keto fried salmon with asparagus *Page: 133*
Wednesday	Keto coffee *Page: 187*	*Leftovers:* Keto fried salmon with asparagus *Page: 133*	Keto fried halloumi cheese with mushrooms *Page: 140*
Thursday	Low-carb mushroom omelet *Page: 90*	*Leftovers:* Keto fried halloumi cheese with mushrooms	Keto fried chicken with cabbage *Page: 104*

		Page: 140	
Friday	No-bread keto breakfast sandwich *Page: 74*	*Leftovers:* Keto fried chicken with cabbage *Page: 104*	Keto salmon-filled avocados *Page: 135*
Saturday	Classic bacon and eggs *Page: 92*	*Leftovers:* Keto salmon-filled avocados *Page: 135*	Keto pork and green pepper stir-fry *Page: 114*
Sunday	Coffee with cream *Page: 189*	*Leftovers:* Keto pork and green pepper stir-fry *Page: 114*	Keto crispy fried chicken *Page: 108*

Week two

	Breakfast	Lunch	Dinner
Monday	Cream Cheese Pancakes *Page: 77*	*Leftovers:* Keto crispy fried chicken *Page: 108*	Keto Cream and Chicken Soup *Page: 106*
Tuesday	Lox omelet *Page: 94*	*Leftovers:* Keto Cream and Chicken Soup *Page: 106*	Spicy shrimp salad *Page: 157*
Wednesday	Keto Mexican scrambled eggs *Page: 96*	*Leftovers:* Spicy shrimp salad *Page: 157*	Keto pizza *Page: 142*
Thursday	Keto Oatmeal *Page: 86*	*Leftovers:* Keto pizza *Page: 142*	Low-carb frittata with fresh spinach *Page: 145*
Friday	Low-carb strawberry smoothie *Page: 183*	*Leftovers:* Low-carb frittata with fresh spinach *Page: 145*	Keto cheeseburger *Page: 124*

Saturday	Spinach and feta breakfast scramble

Page: 98 | Keto Chinese pork stew with cabbage

Page: 116 | Sausage stroganoff with cauliflower and parsley rice

Page: 147 |
| Sunday | Blueberry pancakes

Page: 79 | *Leftovers:* Sausage stroganoff with cauliflower and parsley rice

Page: 147 | Keto pork chops with blue-cheese sauce

Page: 111 |

Week three

	Breakfast	Lunch	Dinner
Monday	Scrambled eggs *Page: 100*	*Leftovers:* Keto pork chops with blue-cheese sauce *Page: 111*	Low-carb Goulash soup *Page: 130*
Tuesday	Scrambled eggs in a mug *Page: 88*	*Leftovers:* Low-carb Goulash soup *Page: 130*	Stuffed peppers with cheese ad ground beef *Page: 127*
Wednesday	Boiled eggs with mayonnaise *Page: 102*	Keto cheese roll-ups *Page: 150*	Keto pork ad green pepper stir-fry *Page: 114*
Thursday	Classic bacon and eggs *Page: 92*	*Leftovers:* Keto pork ad green pepper stir-fry *Page: 114*	Low-carb mushroom soup *Page: 152*
Friday	Low-carb ginger smoothie *Page: 185*	*Leftovers:* Low-carb mushroom soup *Page: 152*	Keto asian beef salad *Page: 160*

Saturday	Low-carb coconut pancakes *Page: 81*	Greek salad *Page: 155*	Keto fried salmon with broccoli and cheese *Page: 137*
Sunday	Low-carb pancakes with berries and whipped cream *Page: 83*	*Leftovers:* Keto fried salmon with broccoli and cheese *Page: 137*	Smoked ham stuffed zucchini boats *Page: 119*

Acknowledgments

I hope you will easily get all the information needed to start changing your life. Honestly want you to be healthy and happy.

First of all, I want to thank my dear wife Sofia and my mother Helen for believing in me. I am thankful to all my readers for the opportunity to present my work.

Hope you enjoyed reading my book!
I would be greatly appreciated
If you could leave your review

"If something is lacking in your perspective—if something is missing in your heart—then despite the most luxurious surroundings, you cannot be happy. However, if you have peace of mind, you can find happiness even under the most difficult circumstances." - Dalai Lama

Wish you all the best. Eat well, love your body, enjoy your life! – Alexander Holt, Healthcare Publishing Author

Made in the USA
Las Vegas, NV
28 October 2023

79872707R00108